SUPPORTING YOUNG PEOPLE THROUGH EVERYDAY CHAOS

by the same author

Working with Anger and Young People
Nick Luxmoore
ISBN 978 1 84310 466 7
eISBN 978 1 84642 538 7

Feeling Like Crap
Young People and the Meaning of Self-Esteem
Nick Luxmoore
ISBN 978 1 84310 682 1
eISBN 978 1 84642 819 7

Essential Listening Skills for Busy School Staff
What to Say When You Don't Know What to Say
Nick Luxmoore
ISBN 978 1 84905 565 9
eISBN 978 1 78450 000 9

School Counsellors Working with Young People and Staff
A Whole-School Approach
Nick Luxmoore
ISBN 978 1 84905 460 7
eISBN 978 0 85700 838 1

SUPPORTING YOUNG PEOPLE THROUGH EVERYDAY CHAOS

Counselling When Things Fall Apart

NICK LUXMOORE

FOREWORD BY JANE CAMPBELL AND
CHRIS MOWLES
PREFACE BY KATHY PETO

Jessica Kingsley Publishers
London and Philadelphia

First published in Great Britain in 2022 by Jessica Kingsley Publishers
An imprint of Hodder & Stoughton Ltd
An Hachette UK Company

2

Trigger Warning: This book mentions anger issues, anxiety,
bullying, sudden death, loss of a loved one.

A CIP catalogue record for this title is available from the
British Library and the Library of Congress

ISBN 978 1 83997 359 8
eISBN 978 1 83997 360 4

Printed and bound in the United States by Integrated Books International

Jessica Kingsley Publishers
Carmelite House
50 Victoria Embankment
London EC4Y 0DZ

www.jkp.com

For Julia
and everyone who loved her

CONTENTS

FOREWORD

This book, *Supporting Young People through Everyday Chaos*, turned out to be the last of 13 books written by Nick Luxmoore, and we wanted to take the opportunity to reflect on his achievements as a tribute to him and his work. This foreword to the posthumous edition is written for all those who knew, admired and loved and worked with Nick, his students, his colleagues, his supervisees, who have had to find their own ways of managing the experience of his untimely and arbitrary death.

In Chapter 2, 'Anxiety and Chaos', Nick wrote these lines:

> 'Everything happens for a reason' describes an illusion of intentionality, a world organised and joined up, a world that makes sense because someone, somewhere is organising it, making sure that it makes sense.

He is commenting on his session with Maya who is 15 and has come to see him as she 'dreads waking up in the morning'. He explores the experience of her anxiety with her with his customary ease and generosity, tries to switch the focus from the symptoms to the possible causes, and sympathises with her disappointment: 'Who wouldn't want a simple solution? Who wouldn't want to escape rather than face the brute realities of life?'

She concludes that there is nothing she can do, 'And anyway, I believe everything happens for a reason, so maybe this was all meant to be.' It is this comment which leads Nick to make his statement about the illusion of intentionality. 'It's an illusion that needs to be challenged, or the consequences for young people can be dire when...the illusion finally breaks down.'

Nick died on the night of Friday 8th November 2019. His death was a great shock to all of us, but sudden death is not unusual for a man of his age. And to respect the hard work that he had already put into this book, we decided to publish it posthumously. He had been at a conference in Cambridge that day, and at home he was in the final stages of preparing this book for his publishers. He embarked on this volume, his most personal book, during the chaos surrounding the similarly unforeseen death of his daughter Julia. As usual, he used his own experiences in creating imaginary young people with their own fictional histories to develop his narratives centred upon chaos and its ramifications. 'Young people might complain that they can't live with chaos, but they know they can't live without it.'

'Everything happens for a reason.' Does it? We, like Maya, long for this response to our grief to be true.

Nick was an inspiring teacher and supervisor and therapist. He lived his work, he lived what he taught. He was able to say, do not do what I say, do what I do. In his determination to reach his patients he took risks. He was 'present in the room' in an exemplary way. He modelled openness, trust, kindness, commitment. He tells an extraordinary story in Chapter 5 which exemplifies this preparedness to put himself out there in an unsafe place for the sake of enabling young people to find their own creativity. It is 1987 and he is working as a youth worker. He wanted to expand the repertoire of the youth centre, including music and drama, 'But the young people I was meeting for the first time hated me... In between our nightly games of pool, darts and table tennis, I would mention the possibility of gigs, of plays, of girls-only groups. They hated me even more.'

His solution was to get up on stage himself. He chose to sing Eric Bogle's anti-war song 'The Green Fields of France'. If you don't know it listen to it now. There are several affecting versions on YouTube. It concerns the arbitrary and untimely death of a 19-year-old boy in WWi. Apart from the poignant lyrics, the sheer musical difficulty of singing this song with its mournful semi-tones and with only a drummer keeping time is astonishing. Nick knew he couldn't sing but 'Somehow I got through to the end, trying to compensate for my musical ugliness at least by *meaning* every word of the song I was singing.' They booed and shouted him off the stage. 'I'm sure I was shit, but that wasn't the point. The point was about people being brave enough to try something different...' Five years later he weeps when he hears a band with its origins at the youth centre playing at a venue in Oxford.

This story tells us more about Nick than almost anything else. He was passionate about his work; but more than that, he was prepared to open himself up to the scorn of his audience if it meant that they ended up braver, less afraid of failure, more open to face the cruel arbitrariness of life with courage.

We gain insight into Nick Luxmoore the man from reflecting on some of the episodes about his own life which he recounts, but we can also experience him through his working methods (counselling and writing), which he developed throughout his oeuvre.

A lot of what follows may be obvious to the counselling community in terms of working practice, but we think it may be worth spelling out the pedagogic intent in his books. Nick started out as a teacher, became a youth worker and then flourished as a counsellor. It was the accumulation of this experience and skills which made him such an exceptional counsellor, but he never lost the enthusiasm for teaching.

Nick was a great communicator and loved language. His ability to capture dialogue in his fictionalised accounts of encounters with clients points to his enhanced skill for deep listening, but also reveals an ear for nuance and ambiguity. The iterative, explorative unfolding of the therapeutic alliance in Nick's consulting room gives a vivid sense of two people hard at work, sifting, testing, trying to develop new meanings together. And although he read widely and in an interdisciplinary way, he never let his learning obstruct the reader. By bringing in literature, philosophy, psychoanalysis, Nick brought in a broader community of inquiry to help illuminate the human dilemma that he was struggling with, with the particular young person. He was scholarly, but in an easy and unobtrusive way. In that sense, he was also pointing to one of the central strengths of the counselling relationship, that we are never alone with our problems simply by attempting to articulate the difficulties of being a human being in constant but sometimes painful relation with others.

Over and over again Nick uses the word 'imagine', as he struggles to see the world as his young person sees it. This is his literary and interpretative gift.

Nick was persistent, not to say stubborn at times, and his accounts of his discussions with young people give a vivid rendering of the counselling relationship; sometimes he returns again and again to the same point, worrying away at it on behalf of both parties in the dyad. He was stubbornly on their side. In episodes in the book, he claims to like the young person and says he believes that they like him; this is easy enough to say, but as a reader we get a felt sense of this liking. His sometimes dogged curiosity is one of the ways that he conveyed it, even to the young people who were harder to reach. He worked easily and skilfully with transference and counter-transference without at all making it obvious in the counselling room.

Nick's enormous humanity shines through in his rapport with the young people. He was able to share a joke when playfulness was required. He was also able to be self-deprecating when it was necessary to deflate his own self-importance. Nick once said that it was vital never to get carried away by your own propaganda, and this insight arose from what he learned from being with young people, who often have enhanced 'bullshit detectors'. And perhaps this was also part of Nick's wisdom as a counsellor and key to establishing a rapport with young people. He was open to being moved and shaped by those he counselled: although the relationship was inevitably asymmetrical in terms of power, it was always equal in terms of respect.

He never glossed over the harshness of life or the pain inherent in the risks of loving. As far as we know, he never measured or quantified anything; what he worked with was a vast compassion, particularly for young people. He quotes from Stephen King's novella *The Body*, about 'four friends on the cusp of adolescence, each of them already scarred by life'. This was his territory, too. King writes of a deer who appears arbitrarily in the night and gazes at the narrator, one of the four, who reflects: 'What I was seeing was some sort of gift... something given with a carelessness that was appalling.' Then Nick adds, 'The "gift" I take to be the appallingly careless and utterly wonderful moment of connection between the boy and the deer, suddenly there and suddenly gone. Like childhood.'

Before writing this book, Nick approached us both, as two of a group of people he used as critical sounding-boards for his texts, about the title and focus of this volume. At first, he had wanted to write about complexity but was a bit wary of getting snagged in technical definitions. Instead he chose to organise the material around the theme of chaos. But in the end, this

his final book and the rest of his oeuvre realises what he fought shy of addressing directly: the ability to sustain complex thinking and engagement with what it means to be a young person learning to develop and stay in painful, yet sometimes joyful relation with others. Nick was critical of simple solutions and reductive thinking, and his work is a testament to the generative complexity of his practice.

Jane Campbell
Chris Mowles
Oxford, February 2020

PREFACE

I'm aware that it's an unusual thing to be doing, writing a preface for my late partner's final book: a work that was written partly in response to the death of our daughter. I wanted to do this because he brought our grief about our daughter into his book, and I know that if he had lived longer we would have continued to discuss our different experiences, and this might have shaped something different.

Among the small group of colleagues, friends and family who read this book in its draft form, there have been two different reactions. Several colleagues found it the most personal of all his books. Others, mostly family members, felt that the transition from the intensely personal first section to the main body of the book is very sudden, and that Nick's own experience of grief should perhaps be threaded through the rest of the book. Frances and I suggested this to Nick when we read the first draft, but he found it hard to continue this thread and to write more about his own grief.

I think perhaps he couldn't write more about his own response to grief, as a key element of this response was to throw himself into his work. He felt that working with young people and those who supported them was the way he wanted to keep connected to Julia, and to a sense of purpose in his life. Many wondered at the way he went back to work so quickly and that he was able to be so fully present for his supervisees. This was also a way of coping and of helping him to compartmentalise his sadness, a way of managing the internal chaos. It was a coping mechanism learned at boarding school: in some ways helpful, in other ways perhaps not.

In his Introduction, Nick writes about the importance of strong and secure early attachments in helping us to recover from potentially devastating events, and in preparing us to live with the constant possibility of chaos, both within and outside of ourselves. Our good fortune in having experienced good attachments and in continuing to be surrounded by generous and loving family and friends enabled us, he felt, to be profoundly distressed, but not traumatised, by Julia's death.

Although the suddenness was appalling and although we were profoundly distressed, Julia's death didn't traumatise us, at least not in a neurological way.

I have wondered about the truth of this, for myself, as I continue to experience the shock of Julia's death, sometimes in quite visceral ways. Perhaps though, these reactions are not traumatised ones, but particularly painful instances of chaos intruding through the carefully woven fabric of everyday life. Even these reactions, sometimes coming suddenly and unexpectedly, become gradually part of continuing life – another aspect of chaos perhaps, alongside memories, gentler sadness and the gradually recovering ability to find joy in new experiences and comfort in former ones.

Helping young people to find ways of living through and with chaos was what Nick saw as the task for himself and for the counsellors he worked with. Writing this book was for him one of those ways: a way of bringing some order and form to his grief, and of helping others to cope with their own experiences of chaos.

Writing this at a time when unexpected global chaos has

engulfed us all, I often wonder what he'd have made of it all. I'm sure he'd have carried on writing, and thinking about how the external chaos and uncertainty is mirrored inside us all, about how we help young people to live with the inner and the outer chaos, and how we live with it ourselves. He would also have been supported, as I have been, by our friends and family and by Julia's friends: all those to whom this book is dedicated.

I'd like to add my own thanks and addition to his dedication: to all those who loved and continue to love Julia, and who loved and continue to love Nick.

Kathy Peto

Acknowledgements

A version of Chapter 10 was published by BACP in the March 2019 issue of the journal *BACP Children, Young People & Families*.

I'm grateful to the following people for reading and commenting on earlier drafts of this book: Kathy Peto, Frances Peto, Dr. Anthony Berendt, Lesley Dewhurst, Mark Dewhurst, Sandra Jay, Debbie Lee, Katia Houghton, Professor Chris Mowles and Jane Campbell.

I'm very grateful to Sarah Knight who organises much of my training work, and to my supervisor, Jane Campbell.

Thanks and love always to Kathy and Frances.

1

INTRODUCTION

On 17th September 2018 our 27-year-old daughter died. She'd been hit by a bus the day before, causing catastrophic injuries to her brain. We stood beside her bed in the critical care unit as doctors performed a final series of tests to confirm that there was absolutely no activity in her brain. Finally, they turned off the machine that was causing her lungs to breathe in and out. Nothing happened. For five minutes we watched her lifeless body lying there, unable to breathe for herself. She was dead.

Growing up, we live with the perpetual threat of life changing suddenly, of our parents abandoning us, of getting lost, losing control, dying. Our fledgling defence mechanisms are forever alert to danger and to unforeseen attack, even when we know that the chances of these things happening are slim. Then, as we get older, we develop more reliable routines, training ourselves to respond in certain ways, should anything untoward occur. In effect, we become more and more practised at keeping chaos at bay, and yet still sometimes it catches us unawares, still sometimes it threatens to crush our sense of ourselves; and when that happens, we either break down and give up, or we find ways of living through the chaos, of living with it, of 'acting into the unknown' (Mowles 2015).

We'd been at home the day before, the sun shining, my

partner writing her dissertation while I mowed the lawn, hoping that this would be the last time it would need mowing before the autumn. The doorbell rang. Two police officers asked us our names before telling us that Julia had been in an accident; that she'd been taken to a hospital in London; that we should go with them immediately.

We sat together in the back of the police car, siren wailing and blue lights flashing, wondering whether she was dead (why else would the police go to all this trouble?) but remembering that we'd spoken to her on the phone only two hours earlier. We wondered what it would be like if she was hospitalised for a long time, about whether we should tell her sister and risk frightening Frances unnecessarily if Julia's injuries turned out to be less serious than we imagined. We asked the police officers if they had any more information. (They hadn't, or weren't saying.) We worried about whether, in our hurry to leave the house, we'd remembered to double-lock the front door and about who would feed the cat. We admired our driver's skill, weaving between other cars swerving out of the way. I worried about not having any shaving equipment with me, about work appointments the next day and about whether I'd be able to get messages to the people I was due to see. We wondered if Julia was in pain, if she knew we were on our way, getting to her as quickly as possible.

The journey from Oxford to the hospital in South London took less than an hour, our thoughts veering between the ridiculously mundane and the unimaginably awful...

This book is about young people struggling to adapt and live with the constant possibility of things breaking down, of normal life being overtaken by chaos. I've worked for over 40 years as a psychotherapist, youth worker and teacher, listening to young people's stories, trying to help them make sense of the chaos they've been describing: chaos at home, chaos with friends, chaos in school. Occasionally they've described the chaos of a sudden death. But however different our personal circumstances may sometimes be, there's no hierarchy of awfulness: finding out that your parents are splitting up or falling out with your best friend can feel as overwhelming as a daughter's death. Chaos is always hard to bear, always hard to understand and always hard to live through.

And chaos isn't only to be found in the unexpected and terrible things that happen to us. Chaos is internal as well as external, a potential that we carry inside ourselves. Freud (1923) famously proposes that our psyche is made up of three elements shifting constantly in dynamic relationship with each other, never still. Buried deep in our unconscious, he suggests, is an 'id': a primitive mass of chaotic impulses, dangerously destructive and likely to usurp our rational minds unless kept firmly in check by a second element, a censorious and powerful 'superego', repressing emotion and critical of anything spontaneous or impulsive. This 'superego' is as tyrannical in its capacity to control our behaviour as the 'id' is tyrannical in its capacity to upset our equilibrium. So a third element is necessary: an 'ego', mediating between the two, trying to maintain some kind of perspective, trying to hold these warring elements in a dynamic amalgam, ensuring that neither gains the upper hand.

Of course no physical id, superego or ego actually exists, but Freud's idea is still useful as a metaphor, as a way of describing what seems to be our experience. It's as if we *seem* to have the capacity to be overtaken by primaeval chaos on the one hand, and as if we *seem* to be prey to voices forever inhibiting and holding us back from chaos on the other. And it's as if we need to develop a mind (an ego), capable of living with and bearing these opposites in a way that's tolerable, because we can't get rid of them – either through nature or nurture they're built into our psyches – and because to some extent we need them. We need the creative, chaotic spontaneity of the id, just as we need the controlling, inhibiting power of the superego. Young people are fascinated by the riot going on in the classroom down the corridor, but they're also admiring of teachers who 'can keep control'. There are some young people who are habitually described as chaotic, unable to control or regulate their impulses and forever at the mercy of turbulent feelings, while there are others crippled by the voices in their heads, forever putting them down, shutting them up, destroying their self-confidence and self-belief.

In my experience, Freud's three-part metaphor is played out constantly in the behaviour of young people, especially in the behaviour that gets them into trouble, makes them unhappy and results in their needing help. That behaviour is almost always an attempt to deal with chaos of one sort or another. So this book is about young people's experience of chaotic things happening to them and of the chaotic id inside them: potentially dangerous and destructive, but also potentially creative. As Wieland-Burston (1992) writes, 'Chaos is a dynamic aspect of all living systems. Without it, organisms would stagnate, or even cease to exist' (p.3). Young people might complain that they can't live with chaos, but they know that they can't live without it. Teenage culture has always veered between the oppressively staid and the uproariously chaotic. I remember the creativity unleashed by punk, when the old rulebook was thrown away and new possibilities emerged, until, years later, those new possibilities in their turn became staid and predictable, in need of another good shake-up. The avant-garde always seems chaotic and meaningless, outrageous at first; it's not until years later that it begins to make sense. 'I tell you,' writes Nietzsche (1961), 'one must have chaos in one, to give birth to a dancing star. I tell you: you still have chaos in you' (p.46).

At a time in our history when young people are encouraged to believe that the world can be made predictable, that life can be regulated and controlled by education, by consumer capitalism, by positive thinking, this book is about the less readily acknowledged part of young people's experience, the part that interrupts their 'progress', causing them to behave in destructive, inappropriate but also potentially creative ways. It's a book about the power, meaning and importance of chaos in their lives, about living through times when, as W.B. Yeats (1961) has it in his poem 'The Second Coming', 'things fall apart'. Julia's death felt like this: as if all we knew was loosened from its moorings into anarchic chaos. And like so many of the young people I've worked with over the years, I found myself asking, 'How can I go on? How can anything ever be the same? How am I supposed to be? From now on, how are *any* of us supposed to be?' We knew that it might take years to answer these questions, lying awake at night, coping with anniversaries, revisiting places and memories, getting used to the ever-present absence in our lives.

During the weeks and months after her death, kind people kept asking how we were: wanting to be supportive, trying to imagine what our lives might be like. Those who were parents had all imagined what it would be like to lose a child. 'How are you? How are you doing?' Their questions were hard to answer: trying to find adequate words and then construct them into sentences. I worried that people might think we were spurning their kindness as we hesitated, tongue-tied, unable to describe what we were experiencing. It was as if chaos defied language (see Chapter 6). Freud's id is, after all, pre-verbal, primordial, connecting us with a time when we were fragmented, inchoate babies, with no ability to think about ourselves: panicking, thrashing about, waiting for someone, waiting for some potential ego to contain our excesses, to help us make sense of ourselves and to give us the beginnings of language. Had we been able to formulate an answer to people's questions, we might have said, 'We don't really know how we are. We've got nothing to compare this with. It's both awful and mundane. It's the end of everything and it isn't. It's completely unprecedented, yet oddly familiar.'

Chaos may be oddly familiar to adults who've had years to get used to its effects and possibilities, but it's relatively unfamiliar and unrehearsed for young people. Although they don't experience their children dying, they do experience multiple losses and other kinds of chaos in their lives, as this book describes (see Chapter 5). At those times it feels to them as if life itself is breaking down, as if all is lost, as if the unthinkable is happening. *Which it is.* Libby, for example, comes to see me because she's never failed at anything before, and now that it's finally happened, now that she's failed for the first time in her life, everything's going wrong, she says, and she can't stop crying. Reece had always thought that his parents would be together, so is distraught at the suddenness of their break-up and is taking his anger out on other people. Annaliese, with fear in her eyes, talks of despair, vengeance, suicide, of feeling betrayed by her father, the one person she'd always thought she could trust. And Darcus was overwhelmed by anger, seemingly from nowhere: anger that ended with his hitting a teacher. He sits in my room, desolate, sobbing, unable to understand what happened. 'I don't know why I did it!'

These young people are all trying to make sense of something they can't name, something with the potential to erupt without warning. Different theorists try to describe this 'something' in different ways. Winnicott (1989) suggests that we have an abiding fear of breaking down but that this fear is 'of a breakdown that has already been experienced' (p.90) because once upon a time, as new-born babies, we were unformed and fragmented, broken down, until gradually we began to put together a sense of ourselves as whole beings. How much of young people's behaviour, therefore, is an attempt to deal with the fear of things breaking down *again*, an attempt to hold themselves together at all costs? Kristeva (1982), for her part, describes what she calls 'abjection' as an experience of something that's 'immoral, sinister, scheming, and shady: a terror that dissembles, a hatred that smiles, a passion that uses the body for barter instead of inflaming it, a debtor who sells you up, a friend who stabs you' (p.4). The 'abject' is something that's both a part of ourselves and apart from ourselves, something we disavow but which is nevertheless within us and capable of disturbing our equilibrium, our sense of self.

Bion (1965) doesn't call it chaos, but identifies 'catastrophic change' as something that can't be thought about, something that can't be understood, yet something that's intrinsic to our sense of ourselves, a kind of psychosis or 'subversion of the order or system of things; it is catastrophic in the sense that it is accompanied by feelings of disaster in the participants [and] it is sudden and violent in an almost physical way' (p.8). Our experience of Julia's death was certainly all of these things, and young people would say the same about their own experiences of chaos: 'This isn't meant to be happening! This is a disaster! This is so fucked up!'

Expanding on Bion's idea, Eigen (1993) describes how

[t]he self is born, evolves, and dissolves with a sense of catastrophe...a free floating sense of catastrophe which is a fundamental term of our existence. It functions as an invariant which can be filled in with a range of more specific contents (dread of birth, death, change, boundlessness, sameness, the predator, castration, disease, burning, drowning, suffocating, falling etc.) One strains to see its face clearly in what can be seen but it grips one blindly from behind the scenes. (pp.217–218)

Fifteen-year-old Lois is gripped by this sense of sudden, incipient catastrophe. She's a perfectionist. 'I've always been like it,' she says. 'I know I'm weird, but I always need to know where everything is, and ever since I was little I've always hated making a mistake. But now I can't seem to enjoy anything any more. I don't even want to go out of the house or see my friends. And I don't know why I don't, but I don't!'

I wonder to myself whether, having held chaos at bay for so long in her life, Lois is now realising that she can't go on like this, that something has to change, that as a 15-year-old person she has to find a way of accommodating the chaos of uncertainty, the potential chaos of sexual love and other strong feelings. It may be that her perfectionism is no longer adequate for the task of dealing with the complexities of the world. As Wieland-Burston (1992) writes, '...it may be only when chaos erupts that we are forced to realize that we have come to a dead-end. Our old, adopted points of view prove insufficient for our present life circumstances. We need to recover the natural flexibility of our personality' (p.106).

The chapters in this book are about supporting young people like Lois The Perfectionist to be more flexible in their responses to the world. Winnicott (1988) observes, 'If development proceeds well the individual becomes able to deceive, to lie, to compromise, to accept conflict as a fact and to abandon extreme ideas of perfection and an opposite to perfection that makes existence intolerable' (pp.137–138). In other words, flexibility matters; but Lois is unable to discover the flexibility that she needs. She's miserable. I imagine people already describing her as 'depressed' because, as Kohut (Elson 1987) suggests, 'A workable definition of mental health may be the capacity to choose from a number of psychic mechanisms according to need' (p.82). This is exactly what Lois can't do.

Lois looks at me as if expecting me to give her the answer.

'Being with friends is difficult,' I say, 'because we never know exactly what they're thinking or how they're going to react.

'It shouldn't be like that, though, should it!' she says. 'Not if they're your friends! You should be looking forward to seeing them!'

I tell her that it's never that simple, that friends can be exciting but scary, that we can love them but also feel let down by them, that they can support us but also turn on us. 'People are a mixture,' I say. 'In fact, life's a mixture...'

It's not what she wants to hear, but I think it's what she needs to hear because, in the long run, shielding her from the potential chaos of life won't be doing her any favours. A midwife friend who works with young mothers was telling me about the mixed blessing of 'birth plans'. Great idea to get young people thinking ahead and thinking practically, she said, but birth plans are problematic when women *of any age* assume that this is what the birth will necessarily be like, taking no account of the fact that circumstances will almost certainly change, making – at the very least – parts of the birth plan obsolete, and taking no account of the psychological chaos that will inevitably kick in during and after the birth of their beautiful baby.

Faced with the prospect of a wholly unknown experience (giving birth, taking an exam, losing a friend...), it's understandable that young people should want to make the unknown as known as possible. The internet may answer many questions but never the ones that young people are asking most desperately: 'Why are so many things going wrong in my life? What will the future be like? Will I be loved?' Whatever our ages, we're in a constant relationship with chaos, fighting to keep it at bay for fear of something happening unexpectedly or for fear that we'll succumb to something buried deep inside ourselves that we can't control.

It's important to distinguish between this everyday sense of chaos and what we mean by 'trauma'. Trauma is an easily misused word, an example of 'concept creep' (Haslam 2016). It's a word sometimes used to spice up and give pathological flavour to what are actually everyday experiences of chaos. Things are said to be 'traumatic' that are merely unfortunate or upsetting, whereas real 'trauma' is a specific experience that penetrates our neurological defences, leaving a legacy that's hard to shift. With trauma, the amygdala remains stuck on high alert, unable to calm down and unable to process whatever's happened (Rothschild 2000; Spring 2016; Van der Kolk 2014; Wilson 2014). Distorted thinking, flashbacks, intrusive thoughts, hyper-vigilance, persistent nightmares, blind panic and a range of physiological effects... These are all symptoms of trauma, of the brain desperately trying (and often failing) to process experience, whereas chaos, however frightening, is part of life: something that we're born with and must live with for the rest of our lives.

I sometimes wonder whether an ability to withstand the agony of 'traumatic' experience might depend on a previously learned ability to live (or not live) with the possibility of everyday chaos. And I wonder whether that, in turn, might depend on the quality of our earliest attachment experiences, strengthening our neural pathways (Eagleman 2016; Hill 2015), knitting us together, helping us to bear ruptures or what Winnicott (1965) calls 'impingements', unexpected occurrences in our lives, safe in the knowledge that the objects of our secure attachment will always be there, helping us to cope when things go wrong and supporting us through unforeseen crises when the world appears to be breaking down, as we always suspected it might and always knew it could. I remember working with young asylum seekers and refugees (Luxmoore 2008), some of whom had enjoyed secure attachment experiences in the earlier parts of their lives. Of course, these experiences hadn't been able to prevent any of the terrible cruelties inflicted on the young people as they fled from war, torture or rape, but their earlier attachment experiences did seem to help them to recover as – together – we were able to remember and take strength from the good relationships they'd internalised before things fell apart: relationships with a loving mother or caring father, with a supportive family or benevolent deity.

Unless we learn to live with the constant possibility of chaos and unless we learn to live with our own potential for chaos, we leave ourselves more susceptible to being traumatised when chaos does strike. As Wieland-Burston (1992) writes, '...when chaos is accepted it can enliven, activate, animate. But, as long as one defends against it, rejecting it, it can lay one flat and drain all of life's energies' (p.42). Although its suddenness was appalling and although we were profoundly distressed, Julia's death didn't traumatise us, at least not in a neurological way. That might have been partly because we'd always known – deep down – that something beyond our control could happen at any time in our lives. It might have been partly because, growing up with the good fortune of relatively secure attachment experiences, we were residually confident that other people would respond to our distress and that we'd eventually find ways of adapting, slowly incorporating the terrible experience of Julia's death into our lives.

Five weeks after her death, I went back to work, partly out of loyalty to the people waiting for me, and partly because of sharing a sense of what I imagine Denise Riley (2019) means when she writes after the death of her son, 'I work to earth my heart' (p.26). Going back to work with young people and with their chaos made absolute sense: working to ground my own chaos and keep it in perspective; working to keep my heart open and not become bitter; working to remember my love for young people. And as I started to work, I started to write this book.

The potential for chaos, for breakdown, for entropy is contained in the most orderly person or organism, the most orderly institution, the most orderly, everyday experience, like writing a dissertation, or mowing a lawn... It's unpredictable. As professionals and parents, we might be able to make some sense of a young person's life *retrospectively*, understanding why certain events might have occurred, but we can never predict the future: there are too many variables, too many unknowns. However much young people might try to cover all bases by reducing their repertoire of behaviours – staying indoors all day, avoiding contact with the world, revising day and night for their exams – they're tormented by the impossibility of ever achieving complete control of their lives and of their futures. They've all had nightmares, so know that weird things go on in their heads. They've all been ill with viruses or vomiting or cuts or broken bones, so know that their bodies are also perfectly capable of letting them down.

However much they may sense some Freudian id, Winnicottian breakdown, Kristevan sense of abjection or Bionian catastrophe lurking within themselves, most young people have (fortunately) yet to experience the terrible actualities of life. Part of any professional's job, therefore, is to support them as they become increasingly aware of these possibilities and of the fact that the world won't be controlled, that other people won't be controlled, just as parts of themselves won't be controlled.

Some respond to these chaotic possibilities with an insistence that, on the contrary, everything *can* be controlled, like Lois trying to control her world through perfectionism. Others respond with a flailing despair at life's unfairnesses, like Annaliese and her talk of suicide. However young people respond and whatever story they're telling, professionals have to think on their feet, adapting to different young people and their different stories. For that reason, the chapters in this book are arranged in no particular thematic order, because as professionals wait for the next young person to arrive, they often have no idea what the next story will be about, except that, underneath everything, it'll be a story about chaos of one sort or another.

Whatever our response to these young people as they arrive, I agree with Cox (1988) that

> [i]n the long run everyone has to come to terms with the chaos within him. Chaos does not cease to exist because its presence is denied. Passive tolerance of chaos is not enough. Once the chaos within has been fully integrated, creative energy is released. As each man makes his own personal compromise with chaos, so it is transmuted into creative chaos, the evidence for which is found in more productive living. This may take the form of greater energy to live, laugh, or love. It may take the form of more overt activity or in a greater capacity to tolerate solitude, stillness and silence. (p.279)

Our relationship with chaos affects everything. Julia's funeral, like all funerals, was another way of trying to deal with the chaos of her death, restoring some kind of order to our lives by making space for everyone who knew her to think about the experience and meaning of what had happened, trying to find the energy, as Cox suggests, to live, laugh and love, to tolerate solitude, stillness and silence. This book describes young people's struggles to think about both the experience and meaning of the chaos that happens to them and the potential for chaos that they carry inside themselves all the time.

2
ANXIETY AND CHAOS

Maya is 15. Like many young people, she says she's come to see me because of anxiety. 'I get anxious about everything!' she complains. 'And it's getting worse! I never used to be like this!'

I ask if anything's happened or changed in her life that might be causing her to feel so anxious.

'Nothing I can think of,' she says, twisting and pulling at strands of her hair. 'The doctor asked me the same thing. I went to the surgery with my mum but my mum told him she can't think of anything either.'

I make a mental note to find out more about Maya's relationship with her mother, who sounds as if she might be important, either as a supportive presence in Maya's life, or as someone whose 'support' might have become part of the problem. There are young people whose 'anxiety' stems from the difficulty of separating from their parents: needing to break free while wanting to stay merged.

'I don't know when it started,' she says, 'but now it's everything! I dread waking up in the morning because of all the things I just *know* are going to start off my anxiety. And then it stops me getting to sleep at night because I'm dreading what it's going to be like when I wake up in the morning!'

'Dread' isn't a word used much in psychotherapeutic theory. Bion (1967) describes the 'nameless terror' that a baby might experience when its anxieties aren't contained, and Yalom (1980) has plenty to say about death anxiety. But 'dread' is a word used regularly by young people. 'I'm dreading these exams... I dread telling people what happened... I'm dreading having to go home... I dread the thought of us splitting up...'

Maya dreads waking up in the morning. I ask if that's what she dreads most in her life.

'Mostly I dread my parents dying,' she says. 'Or if Jonny was going to finish with me because we've been going out for nearly three months now. Or I suppose if something happened to one of my friends...'

I ask what the 'dread' feels like.

'Like something that never goes away,' she says. 'Like the worst thing that could ever happen to you, that you know probably isn't going to happen, but you know it could.'

Kierkegaard (2015) describes what we feel in the face of life's existential givens as 'dread'. (His original 1844 Danish word *angest* is sometimes translated as 'anxiety'.) Since Adam and Eve's first mistake, he argues, we dread the fact that we're capable of doing bad, sinful things; our freedom to choose between good and evil fills us with anxiety; we long to recapture our pre-lapsarian state of innocence (see Chapter 5). So where religion once offered us a consoling narrative of surrender and forgiveness for our sins, a framework for containing our chaos (the Greek *khaos* means 'gaping emptiness'), we're now left staring into the void of our own meaninglessness with nothing to console us, frantically clinging to whatever might give our lives some sense of purpose. Maya might understand this existential dread in terms of her parents dying or breaking up with Jonny or some misfortune befalling a friend, but somehow she has to become accustomed to it, to the constant threat of chaos, to the 'anxiety' she experiences so vividly at the moment. Somehow she has to find a way of living with the potential for bad things to happen to her and has to find a way of living with the panicky, out-of-control thoughts in her head.

I ask what's helped in the past, if anything.

'Nothing!' she says emphatically. 'So now I suppose you're going to say that I've just got to get used to it...?'

She's reading my mind, and yet it would be unkind to say, 'Hey, Maya! Join the rest of the human race! Life's a bitch and then you die!' It would be hurtful and would belittle the seriousness of her concerns.

Anxiety begins at birth. We come out screaming, desperate to be recognised, to attach to other people as fast as possible in order to survive. It's a matter of life and death. If we're able to make secure attachments, our anxiety diminishes, but if our attachments remain insecure, our anxiety is likely to increase (Music 2014). Wilson (2014) describes the effect on the brain and, specifically, on the amygdala of adverse early experiences, which can leave us with a legacy of chronic anxiety: an inability to process everyday threats and uncertainties. In a sense, our birth is our first experience of chaos, and so the way people respond to our screaming during those first formative months of our lives tells us a lot about how we ourselves might respond to chaos in the future: with panic and fear or with thoughtfulness and calm. So far, I know nothing about the early part of Maya's life, or about how her parents might have responded to her anger, fear, despair, dread.

Freud (1920, 1923) argues that we're powered by primitive anxieties of one sort or another all our lives, and that *all* our behaviours, *all* our defence mechanisms, are ways of subsequently trying to deal with these anxieties. Melanie Klein (1946) contends that anxiety begins precisely at the moment of our birth, that it 'arises from the operation of the death instinct within the organism, is felt as fear of annihilation (death) and takes the form of fear of persecution' (p.100). How much is Maya's 'anxiety' therefore a fear of everything breaking down, a fear that might easily overwhelm a neurologically and hormonally vulnerable adolescent? Rollo May (1977) writes, 'Anxiety is the reaction to the threat to any pattern which the individual has developed upon which he feels his safety to depend' (p.163). Without her parents, without Jonny, without her friends, Maya is potentially alone and therefore potentially endangered. That might sound ridiculous to a dispassionate observer, but when Maya's afraid, my guess is that 'endangered' is exactly what she feels. It's not for nothing that so many young people spend so long checking their phones late into the night: checking that they're not alone, that someone is still out there, still awake and thinking about them. Checking again. And checking again... And *still* feeling unsure, *still* knowing that a few sporadic texts are no substitute for lasting attachments.

Unless they've internalised and can take for granted the idea that they're held in mind by other people, even when those people are physically absent, then being alone fills most young people with anxiety. Isolation always serves an effective punishment if its intention is to make young people scared. ('Get to your room!' screams the irate parent. 'You're going to be in isolation for the rest of the day,' announces the teacher, responding to some misdemeanour.) In complaining of 'anxiety', there may be a part of Maya saying, in effect, 'I'm scared! Scared of being alone, scared of people leaving me! Because then it would feel like I've got nothing, like I *am* nothing! It would feel like being dead!'

Anxiety lies in the tension between our internal and external worlds. We know we have to take an exam tomorrow and we know that the stakes are high. We know that people want us to do well and we've listened to their words of encouragement. We know we can resit the exam if necessary... All this is external. What's internal is our fear of failure, of humiliation, of shame, of worthlessness learned long ago, perhaps from early sibling experiences, or from the desolation of a father's rejection, or from no longer feeling worthy of a mother who was only intermittently interested in our early strivings (Cozolino 2016). These experiences are usually internalised and repressed in our unconscious life. But at times we barely manage to keep them under wraps and they spill out, expressed as behaviours intended to make these persistent anxieties go away.

It helps when professionals are interested in the *meaning* of a young person's anxiety, trying to understand it rather than simply rationalise or medicate it away. I think it's helpful to think of 'anxiety' as the word we use to describe a conflict of feelings of some sort, bubbling away inside us. It might be a conflict between the part of us that wants to grow up and the part that wants to remain a child; the part that loves our parents and the part that hates them; the part that wants to engage with life and the part that wants to run away from it. It might be the conflict between how we must appear in public (getting ready for the exam) and how we might feel in private (dreading the exam). The anxiety is caused by the fact that the feelings are conflicted and by our sense that we ought to be feeling one thing rather than the other. Not both. So it helps when young people can identify and describe *both* feelings, often making conscious what was previously unconscious or unspoken. It helps when young people are offered the possibility that *both* feelings are true, *both* feelings are valid, and that feeling conflicted in these ways is normal. Acknowledging such ambivalence is a developmental achievement because it's much easier to deal with anxiety as a child might, by splitting the world simplistically into either good or bad, right or wrong, love or hate.

'I know I have to get used to it,' says Maya, disconsolately.

'But that's easier said than done,' I remind her. 'We might want to get used to it, but at the same time, we might wish it would all just go away...'

'Exactly!' she says. 'Like, I really envy my little brother sometimes because he doesn't have to worry about anything! He just goes out and plays football all the time with his friends. And Dad drives him to matches, and he only has to walk from our house to his school in the mornings. He's never even been on a school bus!'

Moreno (1961) describes anxiety in terms of roles:

Everybody is expected to live up to his official role in life; a teacher is to act as a teacher, a pupil as a pupil, and so forth. But the individual craves to embody far more roles than those he is allowed to act out in life... Every individual is filled with different roles in which he wants to become active and that are present in him in different stages of development. It is from the active pressure which these multiple individual units exert upon the manifest official role that a feeling of anxiety is often produced. (p.63)

I imagine Maya playing her official role as elder daughter, dutiful daughter, responsible daughter, concealing or repressing all the other roles she might like to play: wild daughter, furious daughter, irresponsible daughter, younger daughter. Indeed, she might well like to extend her repertoire to play the role of son rather than daughter, of footballer rather than academic prodigy. But these are guesses.

She goes to see the doctor. She comes to see me. Dressed

very neatly and made up very precisely, she evidently takes great – probably obsessive – care with her appearance, like many other young people who try to control their anxiety by controlling their appearance, their rooms, their eating and other behaviours, finding something objective on which to focus their subjective anxiety. There are some young people whose anxiety changes its focus from week to week, fulminating one week about someone at school, then the next week no longer interested in that but aggrieved instead about a parent, then about the unfairness of exams, then about feeling ill, then about a pet that might be dying, then about having too much homework, and so on.

As far as I know, Maya is still going to school, still engaging with the world, however anxious she may feel about certain things. There are other young people, faced with similar challenges, who retreat into obsessive behaviour or retreat to the safety of their rooms, enacting their anxieties in far more vivid ways than Maya is doing. Steiner (1993) describes what he calls 'psychic retreats' whereby we withdraw, escape or avoid contact with other people:

> Sometimes [these retreats] are so successful that the patient is protected from anxiety, and no difficulty arises as long as the system remains unchallenged. Others remain stuck in the retreat despite the evident suffering it brings, which may be chronic and sustained or masochistic and addictive. (p.3)

Perhaps at some level Maya has retreated and got stuck. She knows she has to move on, but she's scared.

My hypothesis is that the task will be to help her name the conflicting feelings, the roles she's stuck in and the roles (in Moreno's terms) that she 'craves to embody'. Our work will also involve acknowledging that bad things *could* happen in her life:

her parents *could* die, Jonny *could* leave her and something *could* happen to one of her friends. In acknowledging these things, there might be a difficult balance to strike because, like anyone, I want young people to be happy; I don't want Maya to be miserable. Yet it would be unhelpful to pretend to her that she *should* be happy and that, if she isn't, it must be someone's fault. 'Blame the parents! The school! The counsellor! And find a fix quickly – CBT, anti-depressants, mindfulness, coaching, positive psychology, a magician with a magic wand... Whatever it takes. But please do something, *anything*!' Happiness isn't an entitlement. Nor is success. The world has the potential to be both good and bad, and our lives are usually a mixture of the two, at the end of which we die. Finding meaning in our lives is what seems to matter most, not finding perpetual, beaming happiness, which would be lovely but quite unrealistic because misery, misfortune, failure and disappointment are all part of the mix. So of course it's agonising to watch young people like Maya going through miserable times: the break-up of relationships, fall-outs with friends, bad exam results, not getting chosen for a team, a job, a university. It's hard when young people question the point of anything, when they despair and feel like giving up. But it's normal. It's what helps them eventually to make better sense of the world, learning to take responsibility for the things they can control while accepting the things they can't. Learning to live with the inevitability and unpredictability of chaos.

I'm not a believer but I'm always struck by Jesus' words from the Cross, 'My God, my God, why hast thou forsaken me?' Far from holding on to some belief in the essential benevolence of everything, Jesus despairs – at least temporarily – because that's what we do when nothing seems to make sense, when we feel abandoned and afraid. And at those times we need our parents as well as teachers and other professionals to hear and to bear our despair with us. Not to say, 'Cheer up, Jesus! Try to think positively. I can refer you for a bit of CBT if you like!' The danger would be that, in our panic, we suggest to young people that all problems can be fixed. If there *are* fixes, then fine. But one of the jobs of professionals is to remind parents and young people that, unfortunately, life really does suck sometimes.

'It's hard when there are so many things in our lives that we can't change,' I say to Maya, 'when we want everything to go well and when sometimes it doesn't. And when there's nothing we can do about it...'

'I just need help with my anxiety,' she insists, picking at her fingers, ignoring my attempts at any sort of perspective. 'I want to get on with my life – I do! But all this stuff keeps getting in the way!'

'Stuff?'

'Well, like my anxiety,' she says. 'Like I said, it stops me doing anything...'

Understandably, young people are keen to find someone or something to blame for life's difficulties. If Maya didn't have 'my anxiety', she'd probably have to find something else to blame. 'My parents' might fit the bill, or 'my friends', or 'the way I look' or 'teachers who expect too much of me'. Underneath the seeming passivity, the apparent defeatism of so many young people complaining of 'anxiety', there's genuine anger. Even as I hear Maya complaining that her anxiety stops her doing anything, I feel my hackles rise. 'That's too easy,' I want to say to her. 'You can't just blame your anxiety as if it's a *thing* with a mind of its own, controlling you!' I don't say this, but wonder how much my irritation really belongs to Maya, how much her anger gets trapped inside her, caught in a conflict between how she must behave in public (sensible, responsible Maya) and how she sometimes feels in private (furious, wild Maya)? I wonder how much she projects her anger into me so that I end up feeling it, not her? How much she needs me to play the censorious superego, criticising her for being anxious, so that she can continue to play the chaotic id, helplessly, hopelessly anxious: the two of us locked in binary opposition with neither of us therefore able to take on the role of thinking ego, regulating these warring extremes? I wonder, too, how much information is contained in our relationship so far: fractious, suspicious, uncommitted. How much she's effectively saying to me, 'This is what it's like! I can't trust anyone! And I don't want to trust anyone! I don't know what I want from anyone!' Winnicott (1988) notes that 'The chaos in the external world...represents the individual's attempt to show what the inside is like' (p.136).

In my experience with young people who feel anxious, it's always helpful to find the anger in order to give it a voice, in order to give it back its power, because without anger, we're disabled. Maya's sense of herself, of who she's supposed to be, will partly relate to her anger. 'Can I still be kind, responsible Maya if I'm angry? And if I allow myself to be angry, will it overwhelm me? Will I ever be able to go back to being my old self again?' Her earlier remark, 'So now I suppose you're going to say that I've just got to get used to it', might have been her best attempt at being angry with me, although, even as she said it, she was holding back anxiously for fear of upsetting me and earning my disapproval.

It's important to find the anger, but I would go further. Typically, we feel anxious because we feel guilty and our guilt is born of not being what we seem. 'I ought to be and I ought to feel *one thing*, yet I am and I feel something else...' The guilty secret for many young people is their hatred. I've written elsewhere about the importance of hatred for young people who also love (Luxmoore 2009), and about the importance for professionals of helping young people name their hatred in order to detoxify and normalise it, taking away the shame of it and reducing the guilt felt by its owner (Luxmoore 2019). My guess is that Maya doesn't only envy her brother: she *hates* him. And she doesn't only love her parents: she *hates* them. But hatred isn't what 'nice girls' are supposed to feel. It's not how any of us like to think of ourselves, so hatred gets denied, repressed, buried anxiously in a shallow grave. Unless hatred can be acknowledged and understood as inevitable, as the flip-side of love, as *normal*, it becomes a shameful, horrible secret, and young people spend the rest of their lives wondering, 'Is this who I am? A person who hates her parents, her siblings and all sorts of other people who've tried to help her? Is this really me?' Struggling with these questions, the default position of many young people is to conclude, 'I hate myself!'

'Who am I and who am I supposed to be?' are questions at the heart of all young people's anxieties. When the autobiographical story that they've been telling themselves no longer makes sense (Luxmoore 2017), they either enact their resultant anxieties or they go and talk with someone. My hope is that Maya might soon be starting to say to herself, 'That old story about myself as a nice girl, a good girl, is out-of-date. It's not as simple as that any more. I can be nice but I can also be nasty. I can love but I can also hate. I can be good but I can also be bad. And part of me *wants* to be bad!'

In a sense, all young people are – by definition – 'suffering' from anxiety because adolescence is inevitably a time of turbulence. No sooner is a young person's story told than it becomes inadequate, obsolete: things have moved on, they've grown older. Now there are new understandings, new enthusiasms, new certainties, doubts and antagonisms. As Waddell (2018) writes:

> it must be clear that more than at any other developmental stage, during adolescence a person is stirred by the concatenation of internal forces in the personality, physical changes in

the body, and specific pressures from the outside world. The way in which all this is negotiated is rooted in early developmental processes, and they, in turn, importantly depend on the extent to which states of anxiety have been variously modulated, modified... Or, alternatively, evaded from the first. (pp.183–184)

Maya's uneasy relationship with me is probably an example of the way she relates to people more generally, a re-enactment of her earlier attachment experience: fractious, suspicious, uncommitted.

I ask how things have changed over the years. 'It's years since you were a child, Maya, but I guess it might be taking some people a long time to get used to that...'

She thinks about this briefly, then announces, 'My dad! He still thinks I'm a child! He still treats me as if I can't do things for myself, as if I don't already spend *my whole life* doing things for myself!'

I ask how she'd like her father to treat her.

'Like an adult! Like, I know I can be stupid sometimes, and I know sometimes I get into a state about stupid things. But I actually *am* capable of doing things for myself without him telling me what to do all the time. Honestly! He does my head in! Having a go at me all the time!'

I ask what she feels like saying back to this nagging father.

'To be honest, I just want to tell him to fuck off!' she says. Then re-considers, 'But I could never say that...'

'Because?'

'Because I just couldn't. I don't know...'

'Don't know how he'd react? Don't know if he'd listen? Don't know if it would make any difference?'

'All of that,' she says. 'I've just never spoken to him like that.'

I say nothing, letting the idea of swearing at her father

percolate in her mind. Having rehearsed this possibility in our conversation, she may find ways of standing up to her father without necessarily having to swear at him. It occurs to me that insisting on 'my anxiety' and then getting herself taken to the doctor might have been ways in which Maya has obliquely tried to express her dissent, but the objects of that dissent may not necessarily have understood exactly what it was that she was trying to tell them.

I ask what she's thinking.

'I'm thinking that this isn't like what I expected,' she says, sitting forward abruptly. 'I thought you were supposed to be sorting out my anxiety.'

'Like your father sorts things out?'

'God, no!' she exclaims. 'Not like that! He just tells me what to do all the time!'

'But you *don't* want me to tell you what to do?'

'Well, I do in a way,' she concedes.

I tell her that if some great piece of advice existed, I'd share it with her. 'But I imagine you've already had plenty of advice from people, Maya. Most of it's probably been fairly obvious. And maybe you want that and maybe you don't. Maybe you've got mixed feelings about people who think they always know what's best for you...?'

The ways in which adults respond to young people's anxieties and the ways in which they express their own are important. It sounds as if her father tries to rationalise away Maya's anxieties, and when that doesn't work, just keeps nagging. I know little about her mother. Does her mother, like lots of people, medicalise anxiety, taking her daughter off to see the doctor in the expectation of a fix? Does her mother struggle with internal conflicts of her own?

'Mum gets upset when she sees me in a state. She says she doesn't know what to do. She's bought me all these books, but none of them really help that much. It's the usual things – don't drink coffee or alcohol, listen to relaxing music, have a nice bath with candles, go for a run to get yourself tired, do a worry journal...'

I ask whether her mother ever gets anxious.

'All the time!' she says. 'She's been on anti-depressants for as long as I can remember!'

Perhaps unfairly, I imagine an irritable father dispensing advice and a depressed mother panicking. Maya will be aware of these parental models because young people inevitably take note of how adults react to adversity and to moments of crisis. Do they keep a stiff upper-lip? Do they panic? Do they glibly prescribe behavioural solutions to anyone complaining of 'anxiety'? Do they worry that 'anxiety' is a sign of mental illness? And what messages does Maya pick up at school about mental health?

Spooked by the idea of a 'mental health crisis' in young people (see Chapter 4), schools are particularly prone to catastrophising. And that's where counsellors and other pro-fessionals working in schools have an important part to play – not by sitting on the sidelines offering a few carefully chosen observations to a few carefully chosen students, and not by offering themselves up as the only people who understand and care – but by involving themselves fully in the life of a school in order to help the school better contain its anxieties about young people like Maya and like others who are sad, angry, sul-len, unconfident, distracted, panicking, curious about suicide, cutting themselves and doing other risky things: in short, young people who are suffering from adolescence.

Counsellors have to help reduce the catastrophising ten-dency and increase the containing tendency, bearing other people's anxieties with them, because when alarmed teachers and parents like Maya's act out *their* anxieties, young people are likely to do the same. Individual distress occurs not only within a developmental but also within a systemic context. Distressed students will, in part, be representing or expressing something on behalf of the institution as well as on behalf of themselves (Obholzer and Roberts 1994). That institution will be as much the client as the young person, and without a counsellor's support to help teachers keep thinking, the institutional anxiety grows, the waiting list gets longer and the number of frantic referrals to outside agencies only increases.

Maya will be aware of the ways in which the adults in her life react when things go wrong or when chaos threatens. Some of them (perhaps her teachers) will react as her father does, prescribing well-meaning solutions intended to keep the possibility of chaos at arm's length. Others will react as her mother might be doing, unable to contain their own anxieties and making frantic referrals to the so-called 'experts'.

Adolescence is a perpetual dance between order and chaos, between the superego and the id. No sooner do young people establish some kind of order in their lives than they set about disrupting it, as if unable to bear any kind of stasis. A seemingly 'stable' relationship is disrupted by a betrayal; a young person's calm progress is disrupted by a moment of recklessness or by a bad decision ('I don't know what I was thinking!'). Young people who complain of boredom might be describing an excess of order in their lives and wanting to provoke some exciting, chaotic shift.

'So I've just got to get on with it,' Maya says again. 'You're saying that there's nothing I can do to stop myself feeling anxious. It's just the way I am.'

I've said neither of these things. This is Child Maya wanting an adult to give her the answer.

I tell her that it's important to think about the meaning of her anxiety, the feelings that make her anxious. 'In a way, they're more important than the symptoms of your anxiety, Maya, because they're what *causes* the symptoms...'

This isn't what she wants to hear, and I sympathise with her disappointment. Who wouldn't want a simple solution? Who wouldn't want to escape rather than face the brute realities of life?

'In that case,' she says, 'there's nothing I'm going to be able to do about my anxiety because I can't help the way I feel. And anyway, I believe everything happens for a reason, so maybe this was all meant to be.'

It's what so many young people say in response to accidents, deaths and other misfortunes. I ask them what sense they've made of whatever's happened. What was the purpose? What was the point? We wonder whether natural disasters and human cruelties happen for a reason, whether a relative's cancer happened for a reason. And if there was a reason, then what was it? Who decided on the reason?

'Everything happens for a reason' describes an illusion of intentionality, a world organised and joined up, a world that makes sense because someone somewhere is organising it, making sure that it makes sense. It's an illusion that needs to be challenged, or the consequences for young people can be dire when, years later sometimes, the illusion finally breaks down.

Young people like Maya are forever wrestling with a sense of agency, with what they can and can't control in the world, with whether accidents are ever really accidents, with predestination, free will, fate, freedom and the nature of personal responsibility. Sometimes they believe that they can control everything and, at other times, that they can control nothing. It's hard to accept that they might be able to control some things but not others. It's especially hard when Education offers a simple rhetoric. 'Work hard, work harder, work even harder,' says Education, 'and you'll get to control your life.' 'Embrace democracy,' say the politicians, 'and then you – the people – will have control of everything.' 'Get married,' say the clerics, 'and then your love for each other will be secure.'

The idea that 'everything happens for a reason' is simplistic. It denies that things might happen for no reason, that they might sometimes (as young people would say) be 'random'. When the really big things happen – disasters, genocides – it's comforting to believe that there's a purpose behind everything, something that makes meaning out of apparent meaninglessness and futility. But when smaller, everyday things go wrong – when there are no jobs to be had, when lovers break up, when families fight – it's much harder to believe the mantra because these are the things over which young people expect to have control. They've worked hard in school and yet *still* there's no job; they've tried their best and yet *still* their lover leaves them; they've helped out at home and yet *still* their parents are quarrelling.

Kierkegaard (2015) argues that 'anxiety is always to be understood as oriented toward freedom' (p.138). What he means is that we push for autonomy and struggle against all the things that might thwart or frustrate that autonomy. But the struggle makes us anxious. When young people expect to have autonomous control and find that they have none, the belief that 'everything happens for a reason' becomes much harder to sustain, and that's when young people are likely to take revenge on themselves or on the world for seemingly breaking its promise. When adults tell young people 'Anything is possible! You can do anything!' and when young people then discover that this isn't possible and that they can't do anything, it's hard to know who to blame. 'Is it my fault? Or was I sold a false promise?' The disillusionment can be catastrophic as young people fail to live up to their own publicity. It can feel as if chaos has finally erupted. 'I've got anxiety!' they scream. 'Don't you realise that I've got anxiety?'

I ask, 'What if things *don't* always happen for a reason, Maya? What if they're sometimes quite random? Like when people die, or when bad things happen to us?'

She looks away, disappointed, dejected, twisting her hair again. 'You know,' she says, 'this isn't really helping. I think you're actually making me feel worse. I came in here today feeling okay but right now I can feel myself starting to get anxious again...'

This is the attack. This is Maya refusing to collaborate, refusing to share responsibility for our conversation. It's the emotional blackmail of a child saying, 'If you won't let me have my own way, then I'll cry!' Rather than stay with the anxiety of mixed feelings, of the unknown, it's a retreat to the simplicities of childhood where children are ill and grown-ups are supposed to make them better.

Attacked in this way, part of me feels contemptuous. 'Well go and read another self-help book then!' I feel like saying to her. 'If all you want is superficial advice, go online and get some, if you think that'll make any difference! Otherwise, start acting like a grown-up!' Her panic is understandable, though. She *isn't* a grown-up, and even if she were, grown-ups also panic sometimes and also want simplistic solutions to life's complexities. Accepting responsibility for our own lives is always difficult when there's so much that we can't control. For Maya, controlling me or being controlled by me would be much simpler than sharing responsibility with me.

'I imagine you've been through tough times,' I say to her, trying to be conciliatory, 'and it must feel terrible when people don't understand how difficult those times have been. So I respect the fact that you've come here to talk, knowing that I won't have simple solutions...'

'But there must be something!' she interrupts angrily. 'I can't go through the rest of my life like this! Because if I'm going to feel like this for the rest of my life, then I might as well kill myself!'

First, the expectation of a solution. Then the disappointment. Then the attack. And now the panic... Young people want answers and want them quickly. Learning to wait, to bear frustration, takes time, takes practice (Phillips 2012). As T.S. Eliot (1972) famously observes, '...human kind / Cannot bear very much reality' (p.14). It's as if chaos is a child, an anxious baby inside us, afraid that the slightest disturbance will destroy everything. And Maya, at 15 years old, will be getting used to all sorts of disturbances in her life: the demands of school, the unpredictability of friends and enemies, the changing nature of her relationship with her parents, perhaps the possibility of a sexual relationship with Jonny... Her panic is understandable.

'I haven't got a simple answer, Maya. Waking up in the morning *is* scary sometimes when we've got a difficult day ahead. Dealing with people who expect a lot of us is difficult. Dealing with unkind people is difficult. Life's difficult! It usually helps to talk about how we're feeling, and that's what I can offer. No easy answers. No false promises. No bullshit. I'm glad that you take your life seriously because it's precious. And there's lots that we haven't had time to talk about today. But you've been honest and I've been honest. And I'd really like us to keep meeting...'

I wait for her response, not knowing whether I've hit the mark. I *do* want to keep meeting with her because I *do* mean all the things I've just said. But this is a nerve-wracking moment. Am I about to be dismissed as another idiot who doesn't understand, a complete waste of Maya's time? Is our relationship – barely begun – about to end?

She makes a face, unsure about committing herself or appearing enthusiastic in any way. 'I'm not sure,' she says. 'If we were going to meet again, when would it be?'

We have a short conversation about the possible times that

we could both manage. I make it clear that I'm not infinitely flexible and Maya makes it abundantly clear that she's not infinitely flexible either.

But we do meet again, a week or so later. This time, it's at the end of the school day. She comes in, looking uncertain, clearly undecided about whether this second session was such a good idea. In addition to her school bag, she carries a large, rectangular art portfolio.

Immediately I'm interested. I like Storr's (1972) idea about creativity as the resolution of internal conflict and Winnicott's (1964) idea that 'children play to master anxiety' (p.144), so I'm always interested in young people's art, music, reading, acting, writing, sports: whatever form their creativity and playfulness takes, including the creativity of telling a joke or a story, the creativity of making a new friendship or, for that matter, of making a relationship with a counsellor (see Chapter 11).

I ask about the portfolio.

'It's just stuff I've got to do for my exam,' she says. 'Most people think Art's an easy subject, but there's more work to do for Art than for any other exam.'

I ask if I can see some of her work.

'You can if you want,' she says, 'but I warn you, it's not very good. And a lot of it's not finished...'

She unzips the portfolio and thumbs through various pieces doubtfully, deciding what might be presentable. Eventually, she slides out a piece and passes it across to me. 'I did this the other day. It's not very good and it's not completely finished.'

In front of me is a large pastel drawing in shades of blue, flecked with other colours. A girl's full-sized face, delicately shaded, is turned sideways, gazing sadly into the distance. In the background, behind the girl, is a blurry kind of confusion, like a war scene, while ahead of her on the horizon is a ray of sunlight falling on a tiny rural landscape.

'We were doing Picasso last term, which is where I got the whole blue thing from,' she says. 'But obviously, as you can see, I'm not Picasso!'

I'm staggered by the piece. I say it's wonderful, beautiful, intriguing. I ask if it has a name.

'I haven't really thought of anything,' she says. 'It's just what was in my head. Just some ideas. Nothing deep.'

This is what I would expect, Maya batting away my curiosity and insisting that everything is just as it seems, that she should be taken at face value, that anxiety is just anxiety. Nothing more. Nothing deep. And yet she's chosen to show me *this* picture, a picture seemingly full of depth and meaning.

I say that the girl looks sad.

'Do you think so?' she asks. 'Or maybe she's just fed up!'

I say that's certainly possible. 'But she does look sad to me, Maya, as if there's all sorts of crap going on in the background of her life and as if she's dreaming or longing for something peaceful, far away in the distance...'

'It's just a drawing,' she says.

I wonder to myself whether to ask more about the war scene going on behind the girl, or whether that's too obvious a question, too loaded. I could ask about the landscape the girl is gazing towards, drawn in such fine detail. That might be safer.

'It's not about me!' she adds quickly, reading my mind.

I decide not to push my luck. It's enough that she's allowed me to see something as personal as this drawing, which I'm sure is *entirely* about her, even if Maya doesn't know or won't acknowledge it. We can come back to this another time.

I say that it's a stunningly good piece of work.

'I'm glad you like it,' she says. And smiles.

I realise that this is the first time she's smiled at me, that this is as if she's just said, 'I'm glad you like me.' I feel suddenly choked. Maybe that's what this is all about, I wonder to myself.

Maybe that's what Maya's 'anxiety' and the anxiety of so many other young people is all about? 'I want you to like me, and when you don't like me or when I'm not sure, I can't relax, can't sleep, can't enjoy or be sure of anything.'

I ask how her week has been.

She tells me a few stories, complains about her anxiety, and smiles. Again.

3

BULLYING AND CHAOS

O ut of the blue, I received an email from someone I'd been at boarding school with nearly 40 years before, now living in the USA. He'd clearly become very successful in his field. He explained that he'd googled my name and wanted to congratulate me on my work. 'But I've always wanted to say', he went on, 'that when we were at school, you were a bullying cunt!'

He was right. I remembered. Well, not everything – there was a story about my behaviour after we'd left school that I didn't recognise – but the rest was true. I *had* bullied him.

I said I was sorry, hinting that there might have been things going on in my life at the time causing my behaviour, but that I was genuinely sorry.

He replied saying that my apology meant a lot, and over the months that followed we exchanged emails, reminiscing merrily about the bad old days.

Bullying is one way of trying to make chaos go away. Most of us have done it, however subtly, because most of us have been through times when it seemed like the only way of dealing with some perceived threat or internal conflict (Waddell 2018); although at the time we'd never have described our behaviour in such terms as we teased and taunted, punched and persecuted the objects of our displeasure. We may not have liked ourselves for doing it, but we did it anyway. The enduring fascination of *Lord of the Flies* (Golding 1954), written soon after the Holocaust, is that it exposes the chaos inherent in us all, not just in choirboys stranded on a desert island. It describes what we're capable of doing individually and collectively when there's no one and nothing to regulate and contain our chaos. We have the capacity to be monsters as well as saints (Holloway 2008).

In bullying other people, we project the chaotic parts of ourselves onto them – our stupidity, ugliness, weakness, messiness, cowardice – unconsciously hoping to make those parts of ourselves go away by attacking the person to whom we've ascribed these characteristics. In other words, we accuse *other* people of being the very things that we despise in ourselves; we attack in *other* people the qualities we can't bear to recognise in ourselves. 'Where bullying is concerned,' writes Waddell (2018), 'we may be fairly sure that sadomasochism underlies it' (p.104). The young person whose bad and destructive feelings can't be contained by his or her parents will look to find other containers when those feelings become too painful to bear. So getting other people to feel our sense of helplessness or humiliation makes an unconscious kind of sense. 'The scapegoat mechanism', writes Wieland-Burston (1992), 'has been used in many a society as a defence against chaos' (p.47).

Bullying is pernicious. At worst, it destroys people's lives. From calling people names and ostracising them to racist, homophobic and genocidal attacks, we have an endless capacity to inflict cruelty on one another. At the boarding school I mentioned above, bullying was endemic and hierarchical in all the traditional ways described by Gathorne-Hardy (1977), Duffell (2000) and Renton (2017). Older boys enjoyed an unofficial freedom to bully younger boys, with the understanding that, once you were old enough, you'd be able to bully younger boys yourself. At the age of 11 and new to the school, I was herded into the 'Hobbies Room' along with a few of my more robust contemporaries, for what was known – weirdly – as 'bunny taming'. This meant being pushed into the middle of the room and then surrounded by older boys who were free to beat you up. You were on your own. To fight back was considered cowardly because you had to learn to take your punishment without complaint and without flinching. And needless to say, you weren't allowed to complain to any teachers; that would have been the ultimate humiliation and, in any case, most of the teachers would have told you to stop telling tales and toughen up.

It was terrifying: a group of large 13-year-old boys gathered together on an autumn evening to bully a selection of smaller 11-year-old boys.

Anna Freud (2015) notes that, feeling anxious and afraid of another person's aggression, children sometimes defend themselves by imitating the aggressor, thereby becoming aggressive and powerful themselves rather than anxious and afraid. A child might therefore defend him- or herself against feeling powerless by joining the gang and becoming one of the powerful ones, or might defend against feeling exploited by becoming exploitative. So we smaller boys learned quickly. We set up our own bullying hierarchies and started policing ourselves, learning to hide our fear, creating protective families of our own to replace the ones we'd left behind at home. We learned ways of defending ourselves, proud of our ability to withstand bullying even as we inflicted it on our peers. I'm sure that the all-male staffroom was also characterised by bullying. The institutional implication seemed to be that bullying was 'character-building': men and boys all believing what they'd been taught to believe and doing what had been done to them.

For years I've been running training workshops about bullying for professionals who work with young people. How can we reduce bullying? How can we help young people to be kinder to and more tolerant of each other?

Typically, we begin by sharing our experiences of being bullied and of being bullies ourselves before going on to explore a situation in which bullying is happening. I ask a volunteer to pretend to be a bullied young person. We then ask that 'young person' all about his or her life, gradually inviting other members of the group to become the young person's mother, father, siblings. Using their imaginations, each character adds to the evolving family story, which, long before we've even got round to meeting the actual 'bully', invariably indicates that there are already stresses and strains in the young person's family, sapping her confidence or inhibiting her in particular ways. There may be difficulties between her parents; different family members may have become stuck in uncomfortable roles; there may be sibling rivalries and resentments: all of which may have made our protagonist more susceptible to bullying and taken away her ability to defend herself; all of which may have made it harder for her to find the resilience to cope with the hostility of other people. Acknowledging these things doesn't mean blaming the young person or her family for the bullying that's happening. It simply means that – as in *all* families – there are pre-existing dynamics at play. We're the products of our relationships, and we respond to the world in the light of those relationships.

Observing all this, we ask ourselves, 'Should the professional be attending to the person being bullied or to the person accused of bullying?'

Recruiting another volunteer from the group to be the alleged 'bully', we use our imaginations again, finding out about this bullying person's life, adding into the evolving sculpt significant people from his or her life – family members, school friends, teachers... They all tell their stories and – once again – it becomes clear that the alleged bully is bringing another whole set of dynamics to bear on the situation: losses, sadnesses, betrayals, fears. Often the bully complains of feeling bullied herself and admits that the object of her bullying, the victim, represents something that has nothing objectively to do with that poor person. Rather, the bullied person represents something to be envied – a happy family, a successful school life, an apparent self-assurance – or represents something to be feared – difference, aloneness, unconfidence, sexual unease, physical frailty...

Once again we ask ourselves, 'Where does the professional make her intervention? Who's most in need of support? The victim? Her family? The bully? The bully's family? The friends and hangers-on involved? The institution where the bullying is happening?' The answer, of course, is that all these people need support. As does the institution involved.

When it comes to reducing bullying, it's hard for any professional to make a lasting difference because the internal chaos that underpins bullying behaviour is so intrinsic to our lives. It's in everyone and it's in us. I've sat with many young people telling me about being bullied, and I've often felt completely helpless. We've discussed practicalities. We've discussed ways of avoiding the bullies. We've discussed the importance of teachers enforcing punishments when they know that bullying is happening. But these things are never enough: the underlying anxieties must also be addressed. Sitting there, I've had to remind myself that the helplessness I'm feeling probably belongs to the young person, given to me to feel on his or her behalf through the unconscious processes of projective identification so that I can be blamed for not having an obvious, fool-proof answer, and so that the young person can be absolved of responsibility because now the helplessness has become *my* helplessness.

What does make a difference with bullies and with young people who are being bullied is when we address the chaos head-on: in other words, when we explore the young person's own strongest feelings, in particular his or her anger. Helplessness, avoidance and invisibility may be passive reactions to chaos, but chaos itself is vibrant, energetic, overwhelming, alive and dangerous. Chaos is potentially a young person screaming out loud, smashing things up, losing control. Of course, this makes chaos very frightening and makes us want to hide from it, becoming helpless, avoidant and invisible. Yet in hiding away from chaos we hide our own power, our own energy, our own vitality. So I *don't* suggest to a frightened young person damaged by nasty bullying that he should run out into the corridor screaming at his enemies and tear into them with his fists. That would only result in further humiliation and trouble. But I *am* interested in frightened young people developing a closer relationship with the chaotic parts of themselves: a relationship that's less afraid and more robust, more accepting of those disavowed parts of themselves. And I'm equally interested in the bullies developing a closer relationship with the unacceptable, vulnerable, chaotic parts of *themselves*, because then they're less likely to split them off, projecting them onto other people and attacking them in other people.

Alison, for example, sits slumped in her chair, a look of resignation on her 14-year-old face. 'There's nothing I can do,' she insists. 'I've told the teachers and they've done nothing about it, and I've told my parents but I know they'll just go and make everything worse, so I've stopped telling them anything. If they ask, I just say that everything's all right. It isn't, but there's nothing I can do.'

I check some obvious practical possibilities, but Alison says she's already tried these things and they make no difference.

I feel myself succumbing to the physical weight of her

helplessness, to the apparent futility of everything, weighing us down like a fog. I find it hard to keep thinking. Part of me wants to give up.

'You seem like a very calm person,' I observe. 'I imagine people think of you as someone who's patient and quiet, Alison; as someone who keeps her thoughts and feelings to herself even when other people are being horrible to her...'

'Well there's no point in saying anything, is there?' she interrupts. 'That would only make it worse. That would only give them ammunition...'

'But I imagine there are lots of things about you that they don't know,' I go on, trying to resist the fog. 'I imagine they don't know the half of it!'

She asks what I mean.

'I mean the other parts of you. Because although you probably *can* be calm and patient, I imagine there are other parts of you that people have never seen and know nothing about.'

'Not really,' she says, trying her best to kill off the possibility of any new narrative.

'I imagine you can be quite fiery when you choose to be. And loving when you choose to be. And probably a bit mad and wild when you choose to be...'

She looks at me as if I'm completely stupid, and immediately I feel discouraged. Once again, I feel like giving up.

I don't blame her for being defensive, though. When we're feeling scared and when we're being bullied, staying with the devil we know often seems like the best option. Sometimes bullied people will fight to hold on to their persecuted role because the alternative, the possibility of taking on some new role, is even more terrifying.

I remember our daughter Julia (whose death I wrote about at the beginning of this book) when she was small and fed up with our family, bursting into tears and running up to her bedroom where she sat on her bunk bed and proclaimed in a forlorn, high-pitched wail, 'Now *everyone's* done something to me!'

A child's world is usually framed in these terms: people are either with us or against us; the world is made up of either victims or persecutors; experiences are either good or bad; we're either loved or hated, and we either love or hate other people. Most of us move on from this position and are able to understand the world and the people in it as a mixture of good and bad, of the lovable and hateful. But some young people (and some adults) remain stuck, convinced that life is out to get them and that they'll be victimised wherever they are. They never need take responsibility for their own situation, therefore, because it's always someone else's fault. It's a comfortable position to adopt because nothing changes: life stays simple and no one can make us take responsibility for anything. And it's a position that we're all inclined to fall back on when the going gets tough. New ideas, new suggestions are merely new persecutions to be rebuffed because they threaten the simplicity of the victim's world.

But however listless and defeated it may seem, it can be a quietly hostile world. With great determination, with great persistence, Alison refuses to budge, refuses to countenance the possibility of things ever being different. Typically, a victim's helplessness ends up antagonising people wanting to help, who find themselves jumping up and down in frustration, enacting the angry feelings provoked in them by the victim's passivity.

I'm not criticising people who are stuck in the role of victim. I'm trying to describe a state of mind and suggesting that the role of perennial victim can be a roundabout way of persecuting other people, a way of enacting our own (disavowed) hostility towards other people, a way of being angry with them without having to own or take responsibility for our anger.

The fact is that whenever we're faced with a daunting challenge, the temptation to retreat into victimhood is always there ('Now *everyone's* done something to me!'). We may well be frightened of the challenge but we'll also be angry with The World for presenting us with such a challenge. Alison assumes that everything will go wrong, that she won't be able to change anything and that no one will understand the impossibility of her situation. So when people do try to understand, she finds ways of spurning their help, complaining that this isn't the right sort of help, that it's misplaced or doesn't allow for how *really impossible* her situation is. It's as if she's waiting for some great rescuer to come along and save her from having to deal with anything difficult. And perhaps that's what her parents did when she was younger.

'I wonder why bad things like bullying happen to good people, Alison?'

'Because people are mean,' she says quickly, sounding younger than her 14 years. 'Because they don't care.'

'But bad things seem to keep happening,' I go on. 'So what if sometimes it's no one's fault? What if sometimes things happen randomly? What if there's no plan? What if life just happens to us sometimes?'

'I suppose,' she says, 'but then what would be the point?'

'Good question!'

'There's got to be a point...'

'Has there?'

This is at the heart of young people's questioning, of Alison's questioning and of Maya's in the last chapter. Why *do* things happen the way they do? Why don't we always get what we deserve? Is there someone somewhere sorting everything out, allocating life's good and bad experiences? Or is life quite arbitrary? To what extent can we ever control our destinies?

'Maybe there are some things that we can control,' I suggest to her, 'and other things that we definitely can't. But it's really annoying when we can't control everything...'

'Yeah!' she says. 'It's pretty depressing when you think about it. Makes you feel like giving up.'

She's right. It *does* make you feel like giving up. It makes you feel like retreating to the simplicities of childhood where there are only good people and bad people, victims and persecutors. And sometimes it makes you feel like inflicting your victimhood on other people.

Again I suggest to her that, although people might see her as shy and unconfident, she's probably much angrier than they realise and much, much more powerful.

She looks at me, a mischievous glint in her eye. 'You think so?'

'Definitely! I think you're furious, Alison. But if you ever let anyone see that fury, I imagine they'd be shocked. You probably protect them from it because you don't want to upset them, but the fury's definitely there. And the vengefulness! And the passion! And the determination! And the ability to lose it sometimes! And the good sense of humour! But I guess you've learned to hide all these parts of yourself for some reason. Maybe because in the past some people haven't been able to cope with them...'

This is a key moment, at least for today. Have I made it possible for her to acknowledge these parts of herself, or will she still insist on her helplessness, however hostile and furious her particular brand of helplessness happens to be?

She looks at me doubtfully. 'I *am* angry,' she says, 'but only with myself because I can't do anything to stop other people from having a go at me all the time. It's my own fault. I've brought it on myself!'

Many young people who say they hate themselves (never other people) and who habitually blame themselves (never other people), have learned that the only way to contain their chaos is to do it themselves. Their experience has been that other people will be impervious, or will be scared, or will collapse or retaliate in some way if they give expression to the chaos within them: to their fear, their fury, their destructiveness. So these young people learn to stifle their own cries, to control themselves, to become their own parent in a sense, holding back the chaos inside themselves. It's exhausting, and the result is usually a kind of stasis or lifelessness.

I want to hear more about Alison's chaos because I want her to experience the sense of agency that might come with being able to rant and curse, to say terrible things, to fall apart and be held by someone who doesn't mind and who's happy to bear her fear and fury. Chaos fuels our sense of personal agency because of its energy, its vitality. We need our chaos. But like many young people who've been bullied, Alison seems to have lost any sense of agency.

I ask what she'd like to say to the people she protects from her fury and what she'd like to say *back* to the people who doubt and dismiss her, to the people who take away her confidence, to the people who bully her.

'Nothing,' she says immediately. 'There'd be no point.'

'Because...?'

'Because they wouldn't want to know and wouldn't understand even if I did say anything to them!'

'Okay, but just out of curiosity, Alison, what *would* you say?'

She thinks about this. 'I'd ask them how they think it makes other people feel.'

'And they wouldn't be able to answer that. So if you had to *explain* to them how it makes other people feel, what would you say? How *does* it make people feel?'

'Like shit,' she says. 'Like you're pointless, like no one cares about you, like you don't matter.'

I'm about to say something, but she continues...

'Sometimes I imagine having a machine gun – don't think

I'm a psychopath, okay? – and I imagine walking over to where they're all sitting at lunchtime and they see me coming and suddenly realise what's about to happen and you can see them starting to shit themselves. Then I start firing!'

'And if you were firing words at them, what words would you choose?'

She looks doubtful about this. 'Am I allowed to swear?'

I tell her that her ammunition needs to include the most powerful words she's got, including swear words if necessary.

'I'd tell them all to fuck off!' she says with delight. 'I'd tell them that I'm killing them to teach them a lesson they'll never forget. And I'm glad they're shitting themselves because that's how they make other people feel. Because they're cowards and I hate them!'

Her cheeks are flushed, her eyes shining. She sits back in her chair.

4

MENTAL HEALTH AND CHAOS

'This might be a weird question,' says Lennon, looking at me quizzically, 'but do you think I'm normal?'

It's actually a great question because it's the one that young people ask in roundabout ways most of the time. They just don't dare to ask it so explicitly. Like Lennon, they might aspire to normality but remain afraid of madness and fascinated by madness. On the one hand, they're quick to call each other 'lunatic', 'psycho', 'schiz', 'nutter' and variations on that theme. On the other hand, they proudly tell drunken stories about having been 'completely out of it, off my trolley', or they tell angry stories about having 'gone nuts, gone mental'. The idea of being mad is both awful and attractive.

And fascinating. I remember, as a teacher, the popularity of the book in my classroom library about the meaning of dreams. Students would try to remember a dream they'd had, then look up its alleged 'meaning' in the book, keen to discuss whatever they found there. It was as if they suspected that sanity might not be straightforward, that they all had the potential to 'go crazy' or at least dream some extremely weird and interesting dreams. Lennon asks, 'Do you think I'm normal?' but he might just as well be asking, 'Do you think I'm complicated? Do you think there's more to me than people realise?', half-hoping that I'll say, 'Yes, you're very complicated, Lennon! And because you're very complicated, you're very interesting.'

He'd be pleased.

'It's just that I've started wondering why I do things,' he says. 'Why I *really* do them. Because I know I've done some pretty stupid things, but I honestly don't know why. Like when I did that thing with the supply teacher's car, and I knew I shouldn't do it – I knew I'd get into trouble – but I did it anyway! I mean, that's not normal, is it, doing stuff like that?'

Much as they might habitually see mental health in binary terms – you're either ill or you're not – young people know that it's never that simple, that *they're* never that simple. If the idea of 'mental illness' attempts to put a verbal frame around chaos, to stop it spilling out and contaminating our everyday lives, young people know perfectly well that sometimes 'shit happens'. Chaotic shit. Falling-apart shit. And sometimes it keeps happening. They know that, despite everything, there *are* times when they feel desperate and want to run away from home or get themselves expelled from school. There are times when they imagine killing themselves.

'So, do you think I'm normal?'

I ask him what he thinks 'normal' means.

He laughs. 'That's what I'm asking you!'

I say that we're all normal in some ways and not normal in other ways; we're all like other people and we're all different from other people...

'Okay, I get that,' he says, 'but would you say *I'm* normal?'

Like so many other young people, Lennon's asking for feedback and deserves some sort of response. Like his peers, he might want to add, 'Do I have the symptoms of a mental illness? Do you think I could have depression? Do you think I should be taking myself more seriously or less seriously? Because some-times I do feel *really* bad...!'

The campaigners' assertion that 'most mental illnesses begin in adolescence' is regularly trotted out as a warning, as a way of getting adolescent mental health taken seriously, and as a way of getting desperately needed funding for a very impor-tant cause. But as an assertion it's a bit like saying that most patterns of behaviour stem from family relationships, that a lot of unhappiness is rooted in childhood experience or that we inherit many characteristics from our parents. These things are obvious. What makes the assertion unhelpful is when it leads to young people and their parents anxiously looking for diagnosable signs of mental illness in what is normally turbu-lent adolescent behaviour. Have I got something wrong with me? Am I hearing voices? Is my son depressed? Is my daughter suffering from anxiety? A nice juicy psychiatric diagnosis, deliv-ered with apparent certainty, makes everyone feel less anxious.

Of course, we should never be complacent about mental illness. Of course, young people need to be taken seriously and supported warmly and effectively throughout adolescence. But we've started talking of 'mental illness' as if we necessarily know what we mean. Words like 'depression' and 'anxiety' are huge psychiatric generalisations. The fact is that all adolescents like Lennon have wondered whether there's something wrong with them, whether they're normal; they've all wondered what it would be like to be dead, whether they'd be missed. Talk of an 'adolescent mental health crisis' increases their tendency to catastrophise, and then when their behaviours get pathologised and given a label by professionals, they're only too happy to start talking nonchalantly about their 'triggers' and believing the apparent simplicity of a psychiatric diagnosis.

We'd be better off thinking of adolescence *itself* as a state of mental illness, as a state of physical and neurological turbulence, as a state of extreme developmental flux, as a kind of personality disorder from which, fortunately, adolescents are likely to recover, provided that the turbulence is understood as inevitable rather than exceptional, and provided that adults don't rush to pathologise young people's distress with premature labels or medications. Blakemore (2018) describes the complex coming-together of hormonal and environmental factors affecting the adolescent brain: factors that cause every young person at times to seem out of kilter.

And as a brain develops in relation to its environment, so a young person develops in relation to the feedback that he or she receives: feedback approving or disapproving of certain behaviours, feelings, thoughts. Young people need this recognition, this feedback, not only to be sure that they exist and are interesting, but also to be sure that they make sense, that they're not mad. 'Am I understandable?' is another version of Lennon's question. 'Please tell me if I'm understandable! Because if I'm not, then that's frightening because it means I might be mad!'

Chaos is sometimes an absence of other people in our lives. Needing recognition and affirmation, young people will do anything – however disturbing – to make other people take notice, because without the containment of other people's recognition, life is terrifying. A young person like Lennon, worrying about his 'mental health', might also be a young person worrying about himself in relation to other people. 'Am I normal? Am I understandable? Am I mad? Why exactly did I do that thing to the supply teacher's car?' If the chaos of adolescence is all about trying out different identities, different parts of ourselves, seeing what fits, what gets approval and what doesn't, then young people live forever in the tension between sameness and difference, between being like and unlike each other. It therefore makes sense for them either to split off the 'mad', unacceptable, 'other' parts of themselves, vehemently attributing them to other people (and possibly bullying those people), or to believe that malignant viruses with names like 'depression', 'anxiety' and 'personality disorder' have somehow invaded their adolescent selves. 'After all,' they might reasonably conclude, 'I never used to be like this!'

The mental health of young people is *necessarily* chaotic, which is different from having a mental illness or the beginnings of one. It's easy for young people to type questions about their feelings onto a webpage and be told that they might be suffering from any number of mental illnesses with exotic names. And it's easy to extrapolate from that. 'So the reason I did that thing to the supply teacher's car,' Lennon might conclude, 'is because I've got a narcissistic personality disorder or because I've got oppositional defiant disorder or because I'm bi-polar or schizophrenic.'

Instead of splitting off the 'mad', chaotic parts of themselves, attributing them to other people and denouncing them, young people have to learn to accept these unruly parts of themselves. As with Alison in the previous chapter, I've often said to young people who've seemed especially obedient, inhibited or terrified of failure, something like, 'In addition to being obedient and shy and hard-working, all things people already know about you, I imagine that you can also be wild and crazy and can sometimes do mad things!' They purr with pleasure because they know it's true and because they've been waiting and hoping that someone will notice that there's more to them than meets the eye. Young people like their madness if 'mad' means spontaneous, original, unconventional. They get scared if 'mad' means alien, incomprehensible and out of control.

Lennon's still looking at me expectantly.

'I think you're like other people, Lennon, in that you cope with life most of the time and sometimes you find life difficult.

Like other people, you're sometimes up and sometimes down. Sometimes you feel like giving up and sometimes you can't see the point of anything. Sometimes you feel that everything's chaotic and getting out of control. Sometimes you get angry, sometimes you get sad, sometimes you laugh, sometimes you cry. Sometimes really unfair things happen to you. You worry a lot. You get nervous... All these things actually make you the same as other people.'

He looks vaguely reassured.

'What makes you *different* is that no one else has had exactly your life with your childhood and with your parents and with all the things that have happened to you. They've had different lives but they might feel lots of the same things that you feel. So if you're asking me whether you're normal...'

'Which I am!'

'...then I'd say yes and no. And I'd say it's good that you're normal and it's good that you're not normal. I like both parts of you. I think they're both important.'

He looks as if he can't decide whether to kiss me or curse me.

'Fair enough,' he mumbles, 'if you say so. But I still don't get why I did that thing to the teacher's car...'

I remember the incident. He was excluded from school for several days and had to pay for the damage. When the school then suggested to his mother that her son might need a psychiatric assessment, his mother refused to countenance such an idea ('My son's not a psycho!') and walked out of the meeting. The eventual compromise was that Lennon would start meeting with me, the school counsellor.

We ask young people why they did things. 'Why did you scratch the supply teacher's car and then urinate all over it? Because if you don't understand why you did it, if you did it mindlessly, without knowing why, then that's scary because you might have something wrong with you! You might need a psychiatric assessment!'

'We don't always know why we do things,' I say to him. 'Maybe you were angry with the supply teacher, or wanted to know more about her, or maybe even – and this might sound really strange – you damaged her car because you wanted to feel closer to her!'

He recoils. 'You're joking, aren't you? No way! That's weird!'

And so we begin a conversation about how the unconscious might work: that having an unconscious in the first place isn't a sign of being mad; that sometimes we feel both hate *and* love for the same person; that people like supply teachers sometimes powerfully remind us of other people in our lives, and so on.

'Yeah, but why did I have to piss on her car?' he asks. 'That's not normal, is it?'

'It's not what people do,' I assure him. 'It's not a good thing to do, and of course it got you into trouble. Big trouble. If you pissed on my car, I'd want you to get into trouble! So it wasn't a normal thing to do, but feeling secretly angry with someone, or feeling ignored by someone, or wanting to be closer to some-one... Those are normal things that normal people feel.'

Unconvinced, he shakes his head. 'You've got some really weird ideas!'

5

LOSS AND CHAOS

An early spring afternoon. We were in the school canteen area, cleared now of children, with fallen peas and bits of carrot being swept across the floor to make way for the small audience of teachers coming to hear me speak.

I became aware of her standing next to me, broom in hand, as I laid out a selection of books and papers in preparation for the talk I was about to give.

Cautiously, she checked my name, and then, face lighting up, said, 'You were the best teacher I ever had!'

I beamed at this smiling, 50-something-year-old woman standing there with her broom. She told me her name and immediately I remembered: 35 years ago, that enthusiastic, feisty girl who, for two years, had been in one of my Drama classes. I remembered some of the other students from that class as well and some of the performances we'd put on together all those years ago. She remembered too. Transported back, we hugged each other, delighting in our memories.

Then, as if apologising for not having lived up to something, she said tentatively, 'I didn't become an actress, I became a cook...'

It was as if she thought I'd be disappointed that, after all these years, she still wasn't a Hollywood name. I imagined her life now, cooking every day for the children in school, sweeping up the debris from their meals, knowing all their names and probably most of their parents, consoling them when they cried, telling them off when they threw food. I imagined her having children of her own, teenagers if not adults by now, loving their mum and starting jobs themselves, inheriting her enthusiasm and feistiness. I imagined her out with her friends at weekends, drinking wine together and laughing, telling crazy stories: a group of women supporting each other over the years through the deaths of parents, through marital break-ups and difficulties with children, advising each other about problems at work and how to deal with stupid men. I imagined her telling her friends that – guess what! – she'd met her old Drama teacher in the canteen at school and – what's more – he'd remembered her. 'That teacher! The one we used to have for Drama! The one we used to do plays with! I recognised him even though his hair's completely white... Yeah, *that* one! He was all right, he was. We used to have a laugh. Anyway, I saw him the other day and we had a nice chat.'

'I didn't become an actress, I became a cook...'

I was touched that she'd even thought of acting. As a teacher, I'd never expected my students to become actresses. I'd simply hoped that they'd be kind and confident, whatever they ended up doing. 'And I didn't become a famous Drama teacher,' I felt like saying. 'I became some bloke who goes round giving talks.'

People were starting to arrive. She had to finish sweeping the floor and I had to finish laying out my papers.

Later, with an audience of teachers in front of me, I saw a familiar figure crossing behind them, leaving the building: job done for another day, on her way home, or off to another job.

She smiled. And waved.

Do our lives disappoint us or free us from our dreams? I don't know what this former pupil of mine felt about her life, looking back: whether she cursed the opportunities not taken, or felt proud of her work and of her family, if she had one. I don't know whether she wished she could start all over again, or was glad that her younger days were behind her. I *do* know that a lot of the psychological chaos young people experience is focused on the tension between childhood and adolescence, between innocence and experience, between the life they dream about and the life they find themselves living. When young people are most distressed, that's when they feel the mismatch most acutely, as if something has been taken away for no reason. 'Did I do something wrong?' they ask themselves, in effect. 'Is the world out to get me? Why does everything have to be so fucked up?'

'It is especially easy for us to belittle the effect of loss on the young...', writes Winnicott (1996). 'But loss of parent, or friend, or pet, or special toy, may take away the whole point of living' (p.47). In my experience, all therapy with young people is about finding an accommodation with a pervasive sense of loss, expressed in a thousand oblique ways... 'Why do I have to get up in the mornings? Why do I have to go to school? Why do I have to organise myself? Why are my parents so useless? Why does everything have to be so *difficult*?' Having been ejected from some half-remembered paradise into a midwife's waiting hands, it's as if young people are bereaved, their grief expressed in the same ways outlined by Kübler-Ross (1969) in writing about bereavement: denial, anger, bargaining, depression and – maybe at some point in the future – acceptance. This isn't an experience of chaos erupting suddenly. Rather, it's a slow and persistent chaos, seeping into everything, affecting everything. 'Why can't my life be the way it used to be? Why can't things be simple?' Growing older may be exciting in some ways, but also feels like losing so much: losing simplicities ('I thought my parents would *know*!'), losing play-time ('Everything's really *boring* nowadays!'), losing physical affection ('We're not close any more!'), losing primary school ('I still miss it in some ways'), losing trust in the world and in oneself as a person with straight-forward wants and needs ('Actually, I'm quite complicated!').

Life begins with loss, or with what Lacan (1966) calls 'primordial discord'. As babies, we emerge into a chaotic world of frustration, mixed feelings and disappointment. Things are never the same again. Young people may try to compensate by replacing lost objects with transitional ones (Winnicott 1965); they may replace parents with friends; they may replace an original response with a learned adaptation, but the underlying sense of something having been lost is always there and is always being mourned during adolescence, as if young people – over and over again – are replaying their original loss of a womb.

Indeed, adolescence might be described as the search for a lost paradise, and as a gradual realisation that – after much misery and disillusionment – this lost paradise will never be found. As Holloway (2008) writes, 'All our paradises are lost paradises' (p.136). Bedrooms sometimes fill up with the clutter of childhood because to throw anything away is to acknowledge that childhood is over, that it's time to let go of the dream and take responsibility for creating our own lives. Our biographers are no longer waiting eagerly outside the bedroom door!

But this realisation or acknowledgement is made difficult when dreams and aspirations are promoted as the things that give meaning to our lives. Young people are repeatedly encouraged never to let go of their dreams by adults who mean to be encouraging and want to affirm the potential of every young person to 'succeed'. At worst, these young people end up being told that their dreams *will* come true as long as they work hard and never give up. 'You must be excited about the future... You've got your whole life ahead of you... Your future's so bright... Think how much potential you've got!'

So why do these well-meaning entreaties fall on so many deaf ears? Why do these encouragements so often fail to inspire young people in the ways that they're intended? It's hard for young people to talk about the part of themselves that *isn't* looking forward to the future. They're surrounded by adults – usually with their own sense of unfulfilled potential – urging them on, expecting them to be eager, excited. So it sounds cowardly to say that you're dreading the changes, and yet dread is what most young people feel, in part. Caught between the past and the future, some find themselves panicking, regressing, refusing to take responsibility and insisting that their parents and teachers should still be looking after them, making things simple. Then these same young people are accused of behaving like children and shamed for not facing the future with unbounded confidence and desire.

As I mentioned in Chapter 2, Kierkegaard's (2015) idea of 'dread' is that, even in our innocence, we dread those things unknown, those things that don't exist but are merely possible. So having freedom in their lives is scary, is paralysing for some young people because of all that could go wrong. They're 'condemned to be free' in Sartre's (1943) phrase. Of course, they have the potential to do good things, but they also have the potential to fail, to make really bad choices. Either way, they have no idea what the future will hold and no amount of relentless encouragement and positive thinking stops that being terrifying at times. 'I'd rather not have all this freedom,' many young people are effectively saying as they complain of 'anxiety' or refuse to engage with school, with relationships, with the future. 'I'd rather be told what to do. I'd rather give up my freedom to choose and just stay in bed and hope that this whole business about the future goes away!'

The problem with the future isn't only the prospect of climate change, war, unemployment or any of the other daunting challenges young people face. There have always been challenges. It's a deeper, developmental dread that we underestimate in young people. And adults are part of the problem because we can't help envying young people their youth, their potential. We maintain that – unlike ours – their futures will be glorious, provided that they commit themselves and do the hard work now. So as the school year progresses, we urge them on, part-cajoling, part-threatening. The future is both a promise and a threat. How good things could be! How bad things could be! Towards the end of the year, students get ready for various transitions – leaving school or moving up a year, moving to different buildings, moving on to different courses – and, as with all transitions, their feelings are mixed. For most, there's a part of them looking forward with excitement (or at least curiosity) to the future. But there's another part looking ahead fearfully, dreading the change, wanting to stay put or to go backwards. Over the years, I've known many young people coming towards the end of their time in school who find themselves wishing that they could start all over again. 'If I had the chance to start again, I'd do loads of work! I'd be friends with loads more people! I'd have a go at everything!' It's as if they're asking for the future to be postponed.

I'm on their side because I think that the future *is* scary – it involves losses as well as gains – and that, however much we pretend otherwise, we all have mixed feelings about it. Telling young people that the future is bright and that everything will be fine isn't very reassuring.

'How do you know that everything will be fine?'

'I don't.'

'Well don't say it then! I'm not a child!'

I don't blame adults for wanting to encourage young people or for wanting them to be as happy as possible. In treating them as naive children, we keep ourselves in role as wise parents, and that may often be our unconscious motivation as we urge them ever onwards. Allowing them to be disappointed might feel like another kind of separation. So in order for the future not to be overly daunting and for young people not to give up before they've even started, I think the loss young people experience has to be acknowledged, otherwise that optimistic future on offer remains quite ungrounded in reality. And young people know it. As I've written elsewhere (Luxmoore 2017), the rhetoric aimed at young people about the moral desirability of 'success' needs to be tempered with an acknowledgement that, along the way, failure will be inevitable. Sometimes relationships will break down; exams will go wrong; interviews and auditions will be unsuccessful. Sometimes our strivings won't be rewarded and we *won't* always get what we deserve. These things need to be acknowledged because, for some young people, failure – when it happens – feels like a catastrophic loss. 'Who will I be if I fail these exams? Who am I any longer if the two of us break up? Who am I if I can't do the very thing I've always dreamed of doing?' It can feel like an annihilation, whereby an original sense of self, perhaps built on shaky, aspirational foundations ('I'm going to go to university! We're always going to be together! I'm going to work hard and get a good job!') is now seemingly destroyed by the fact of failure ('It feels like I'm nothing now, like I don't exist any more!').

Therapists would call such a feeling of failure a 'narcissistic wound', an early injury to a child's grandiosity, a developmental reminder that the world won't allow itself to be controlled by the child.

Twelve-year-old Zak would simply call it 'shit'. 'Why can't they make an exception?' he rages. 'I forgot to go; that's not such a big deal! I don't see why they can't give me another chance?'

Despite being reminded, he missed his audition. He won't be appearing in the school show.

'It's not fair!' he says. 'They all know I want to be a singer. It's all I ever think about... God, this is so shit!'

But he's missed his audition and the teachers won't budge. They've made their rule and they're sticking to it. Zak is learning a painful lesson that, however much he might want to be a singer, rules have to be obeyed and the show is bigger than any one person. But of course this isn't his first setback. It's the latest incarnation of something that happened much earlier in his life when his father left his mother and refused to come back, despite Zak's pleading. Zak carries this wound inside himself, causing him to question whether he'll ever be good enough, whether his father really loves him and whether the world is determined to deprive and frustrate him at every turn. I wonder to myself whether he 'forgot' to go to the audition because – unconsciously – he was wondering whether *this time* the world would make an exception, whether *this time* his pleas would be heard. What Freud (1914b) calls 'repetition compulsion' is when

> the patient does not remember anything of what he has forgotten and repressed, but acts it out. He reproduces it not as a memory but as an action; he *repeats* it, without, of course, knowing that he is repeating it. (p.150)

Freud's suggestion is that we keep going back to unresolved situations in an unconscious attempt eventually to master them. And certainly, there are many young people like Zak whose apparently childlike behaviour seems to be an unconscious attempt to resolve something that happened to them *as a child*. It would be no use pointing out to Zak that he received several reminders about the exact time and place of the audition. This was never just about an audition, I suspect, but about something much more important: Zak's loss of his father's unconditional love and the chaos that erupted in his life when he was six years old. *That's* what we need to talk about.

'He never explained his reasons, Zak...?'

He shakes his head. 'He just said that him and Mum couldn't get on with each other any more. And when I said, "What about me?", he said we'd still be seeing each other so nothing was going to change.'

'But it did?'

'Everything changed!'

'And there was nothing you could do...'

He looks at me, as if asking whether there was something he should have done and, by implication, whether there's something he should be doing now to get himself included in the show.

'It's shit,' he repeats. 'Total shit!'

'It's really hard when things change,' I say to him, 'and there's nothing we can do about it. Hard to understand why things happen like that. Hard when we've lost someone, and it just *happens*, and we can't change anything.'

A young person's rage is usually tinged with narcissism, with a residual sense of how things were supposed to be in the beginning. Where once a grandiose baby might have felt able to control the world, now a personal fallibility seems to have crept into everything. 'Why?' young people ask in all sorts of roundabout ways. 'Why is this happening? Why? Who am I supposed to be if I'm not the old me? It's not fair! I've been betrayed! It's someone's fault!' Rage is an attempted solution, a way of dealing with the loss and with the ensuing developmental panic. Find someone to blame! Quickly! There must be *someone* to blame!

Typically, chaos precipitates a loss of imagination. We close in on ourselves. We shut down. We can't think straight. In fact, we can't think at all. So therapists have to re-awaken young people's imaginations, helping them find the courage to imagine again, to imagine what *could* be, knowing that nothing lasts for ever and that whatever they imagine could be swept away at any time. Together, Zak and I have to start imagining again, like a baby and its care-giver, creating a relationship, creating new stories, new perspectives, new possibilities. 'It is in playing and only in playing', writes Winnicott (1971), 'that the individual child or adult is able to be creative and to use the whole personality, and it is only in being creative that the individual discovers the self' (p.54).

'I wonder if you and your dad will get closer in the future, Zak?'

'Doubt it!' he says. 'My dad's more interested in his girlfriend and her kids.'

'But you were his first child,' I remind him. 'You were the baby that he held in his arms. You were the one that he boasted about to his mates. His first-born. You were the one!'

'I know, but that's in the past,' he says bitterly. 'I don't think he's going to suddenly start taking an interest now, is he!'

'Maybe you'll be interested in him,' I suggest. 'After all, half of you is him! It's interesting to wonder where you get your musical ability from, for example. And your sense of humour. And your friendliness. And your ability to get angry and stick up for yourself... Some of these things probably come from your dad.'

His silence tells me that I'm onto something.

'I wonder what he was like when he was your age? Whether he was close to his father...?'

Zak's hurt and it's hard to move on when we're hurt. In desperation, Shakespeare's Othello bemoans the fact that '...when I love thee not / Chaos is come again' (*Othello* III.3.91–2), while young people complain, 'I hate goodbyes! I'm no good at endings!' because endings feel like losses and because the finality is so hard to bear. The hurt, the loss stops us in our tracks, stops us thinking, stops us imagining. Sometimes chaos feels like the loss of love's possibility, and yet out of chaos can come creativity: new possibilities, new consolations can emerge. Sometimes people break down when their old ways of living are no longer sustainable. And sometimes this has to happen in order for them to rebuild their lives on more flexible foundations, living through the chaos in order to find new ways of being. Winnicott (1971) describes how, through this kind of 'playing', 'the individual can come together and exist as a unit, not as a defence against anxiety but as an expression of I AM, I am alive, I am myself. From this position, everything is creative' (p.56).

But even when young people find themselves living in oppressive or joyless cultures, the possibility of doing things differently remains daunting. I'm at the Oxford Venue, for example. It's 1992. As a music venue, it's currently half-way between the dive it once was and the soulless corporate hub it'll become in a few years' time. Most of the audience is here to see a local band called On a Friday, who've recently changed their name to Radiohead, and tonight, as part of their set, they're recording a live video for their first single, 'Creep', which will go on to sell all around the world and, over the next few years, help to establish Radiohead as one the world's most famous bands.

But like several others in the audience, I'm not really here to see Radiohead. I'm here to see The Daisies who are supporting them, and The Daisies – we all sense – are about to come on stage...

The story begins five years earlier. Feeling fed up and trapped, I'd resigned my teaching post in a school and taught in a prison for a year while making my first forays into youth work, co-writing and directing rock musicals in the town where I'd been teaching, thereby getting to work with my ex-students but no longer having to teach them capital letters and full-stops.

At the end of that year, I started a job elsewhere as a half-time youth worker and half-time school counsellor.

I was keen that the youth centre I found myself running should expand its creative repertoire beyond desultory discos, pool, darts and table tennis, and develop a culture that included music and drama and all sorts of other, more creative, more ambitious things.

But the young people I was meeting for the first time hated me. They'd never done any of these things. In between our nightly games of pool, darts and table tennis, I would mention the possibility of gigs, of plays, of girls-only groups. They hated me even more.

Eventually a handful of young people admitted to being in a covers band, and so we arranged an evening that would be half live music from the covers band and half disco, with the disco coming after the band, so that – with a strict curfew in place – the audience had to endure the live band if they wanted still to be there for the disco.

Although at the time their hatred hurt, I understood that part of it was because they were scared, clinging to what they knew, afraid of the unknown. The prospect of anyone being on stage in front of anyone else was scary: not something they could ever imagine themselves doing, however much I might encourage or cajole them. So I decided that I needed to put my money where my mouth was and get on stage and do something myself.

I can't sing. However, this was 1987, the DIY punk ethic was still alive, and I had to have the guts to do these things myself if I was ever going to encourage much less confident young people to risk going on stage themselves.

The half-gig, half-disco evening happened the day after Margaret Thatcher's dreadful government had been re-elected. With about 80 bemused young people watching, I stepped on stage after the covers band had finished and, with a drummer keeping time, tried to sing – unaccompanied – Eric Bogle's furious anti-war song, 'The Green Fields of France'.

They shouted. They laughed. They booed. They screamed at me to get off. A few were silent and embarrassed, listening guiltily to what must have been a truly awful sound. Somehow I got through to the end, trying to compensate for my musical ugliness at least by *meaning* every word of the song I was singing. And I did mean it.

'Get off! You can't sing! We want the disco! You're shit!'

I'm sure I was shit, but that wasn't the point. The point was about people being brave enough to try something different and I guessed that, secretly, there would be a few young people in the audience who fancied themselves as musicians.

One of them turned out to be Jamie. I remember him as one of the cynics, smoking at the back of the darkened youth centre, probably shouting and sneering with his friends at the spectacle of a grown man with no musical ability trying to sing.

Over the next few years we did more and more music at the youth centre. We continued to run discos as well, and gradually I began to understand how exciting and politically important a well-run disco can be, proving to young people that it's possible to come together and have fun *en masse* without anyone bullying anyone else or spoiling the event. But we also convened an increasing number of free-standing gigs with bands we brought in to play. We started a youth centre gig committee, charged with booking and running the gigs. We bought a smoke-machine and lights. We bought our own PA system. And gradually more and more people started admitting to playing a bit of guitar or having a drum kit or being tentatively interested in singing. The gigs were packed.

I can't remember exactly how Jamie and his friends did it but, as others were doing, they formed a band, and my job was to provide them with instruments and arrange places for them to practise. That band were unusual in that, unlike the other fledgling bands thrashing away in the youth centre, you didn't hear pointless guitar noise coming out of their practice room. If Jamie's band were working on a song, they played it over and over again, night after night, getting tighter and tighter musically and only adding vocals once the basics were secure.

Five years later... The Oxford Venue is dark, full of smoke and excitement with three hundred people crammed in, sipping beer, enthusiastically greeting each other and straining to see the stage.

I confess that some of the most exciting, uplifting experiences of my life have been at rock concerts with the sense of people coming together to support the band, the catharsis of big guitar chords breaking into choruses, the excitement of recognising the first bars of the next song with the audience willing the band along, wanting them to be wonderful.

The Daisies are finally on stage and they're wonderful: confident and tight, attacking their songs and pulling us together, making us feel that we share a purpose, bound together and driven by the music. When Radiohead come on later, they'll sound restrained and awkward, as if still searching for an identity. And in the middle of 'Creep' the singer will start coughing.

But for now I stand at the back of the crowd, watching Jamie and his friends on stage. The Daisies from the youth centre! A year from now, they'll go on to tour America in support of Supergrass, then tour Japan in their own right, and in the meantime their first album will come out: songs developed in the practice rooms of the youth centre, sitting round on benches, night after night, getting tighter and tighter.

I think back a few years and weep, knowing that it's been worthwhile.

New experiences may be exciting, but they're also always

frightening. Once upon a time there was order, however constraining it might have been, and now there's the chaos of the unknown. The past may have had its limitations but at least it was familiar. Young people know that they can't go back, but at the same time, they're afraid of going forwards.

Stephen King's novella *The Body* (1982/2018), also made into the film *Stand by Me* (Reiner 1986), tells the story of four friends on the cusp of adolescence, each of them already scarred by life. They decide to go in search of a missing older boy whose dead body, they've heard, is to be found beside the railway tracks several miles away. They set off along the railway line, symbolically journeying from innocence to experience, vaguely aware of what awaits them, fascinated and frightened, but driven to confront this rite of passage.

Along the way, they joke and argue, get into scrapes and extricate themselves from scrapes. Eventually, they find the boy's body and, later, trudge home, chastened but calmer. They've stopped joking. They've stopped arguing.

But although finding the boy's body is the focus of their adventure, the crucial moment in the story occurs earlier when the narrating boy is sitting alone by the railway line while his friends sleep. Suddenly a deer appears. It stands gazing at him, seemingly unconcerned by his presence. There's a fleeting moment of recognition, of meeting between the boy and the deer before the deer vanishes as suddenly as it appeared. 'What I was seeing was some sort of gift,' the boy reflects, 'something given with a carelessness that was appalling' (p.123).

At the end of the story, we learn of the unconnected deaths, years later, of his three friends – now grown men – in a fire, a car crash and a stabbing: deaths happening with appalling carelessness. The 'gift' I take to be the appallingly careless and utterly wonderful moment of connection between the boy and the deer, suddenly there and suddenly gone. Like childhood.

6

LANGUAGE
AND CHAOS

There's a marvellously creepy song by Tom Waits (1999) called 'What's He Building?' in which the narrator speculates endlessly about what might be going on inside the house of a neighbour nobody knows anything about, a neighbour who never comes out of his house and seems to have no friends, a neighbour about whom all sorts of rumours are circulating. Is he keeping someone prisoner? Is he planning an attack? Is he communicating with aliens? There are noises coming from inside the house... What's he building in there?

We get paranoid about countries and about people we don't understand, just as we're wary of young people who don't talk. How should we interpret their silence? Are they choosing not to speak? Are they shy? Are they biding their time? Are they about to explode? What exactly is going on?

Alwyn sits back in his chair, frustrated, fed up with himself and fed up with me. 'I don't know how to say it!'

He's trying to talk about his mother, about their relationship since his father left and since her boyfriend moved in. This year has been especially difficult. Alwyn is 13 now and has started getting into all sorts of trouble at school, taking his anger out on female teachers in particular.

He remembers his father hitting his mother when he was small. He remembers being locked in his bedroom while it was happening and remembers being let out eventually to find his mother half-dressed, alone with her phone, saying nothing and taking no notice of him, his father having left the flat to go drinking. He remembers not knowing what to say or do, so going back to his room, sitting on the bed and playing games online for hours to distract himself. He was five years old.

In our earlier meetings, he's managed to tell me these things, but in a jumbled up way, out of sequence, the two of us trying to piece the information together chronologically, trying to make a more coherent narrative.

'I don't know,' he manages to say in answer to my question about how things are at the moment between him and his mother. 'I don't really feel anything.'

He might mean that he can't speak for fear of being overwhelmed. He might mean that he has no words for the maelstrom of powerful, contradictory feelings almost certainly locked up inside him. The trouble is that some of these feelings are starting to spill out in his relationships with women at school where his behaviour is getting him into serious trouble.

I'm not surprised that he struggles to speak. When he was five, he was locked away in his bedroom and silenced. And when he was finally allowed out, no one was listening, his mother locked away in her own world, still alive but unable to look after her son, unable to explain to him what had just happened, unable to help him make sense of the chaos unleashed by a violent father choosing to believe that Alwyn's mother was having an affair.

It's frustrating for professionals, sitting with young people who say nothing, young people who are monosyllabic or who keep saying 'I don't know!' in answer to every question. It makes us question our competence and question a young person's motivation in being with us ('Do you really want to be here?'). We wonder whether somebody else on the waiting list wouldn't be getting more out of this opportunity to talk. There are young people who choose not to talk or who simply refuse to talk as their best way of protecting themselves. But there are young people who *can't* talk, who can't describe what they're experiencing when primitive chaos overwhelms them and they're terrified (Luxmoore 2019). So they shut down, hoping that the listener will persist, prompting them, second-guessing what it is that they might be experiencing, bringing them back to normality with words, lifting them out of chaos with the help of language. This is close to what Bion (1963) calls 'containment': the listener's ability to hear a young person's unending, painful silence or panic-stricken howl and give it a name, give it words that make sense, give it meaning. In short, the listener contains and recognises what the young person is experiencing and, in so doing, brings the young person back from the brink of what feels like madness.

From his bedroom, Alwyn heard his father beating up his mother. When chaos strikes, it can take away our language and leave us speechless. It's as if we regress, as if the external chaos makes contact with the residual, unconscious, pre-verbal chaos inside us. In the beginning, as babies, we lived with that chaos and began to create order out of it by discovering bits of language that structured our otherwise chaotic experience. Initially, we did this by making noises to signify our experience (a howl, a whimper, a chuckle), noises that were then shaped by an attuned, attentive parent or carer into recognisable, repeatable sounds called words and offered back to us, words gradually developing through these interactions into sequences called sentences and exchanged between ourselves and other people as meaning (Stern 1985).

When external chaos happens (in Alwyn's case, his father hitting his mother) and we're temporarily overwhelmed, we're likely to regress to that internal, pre-verbal state. Things stop making sense. Words fail us. We can no longer think. 'I don't know how to say it!' complains Alwyn.

Typically, young people begin therapy unsure what to say or how to say it. They tell stories that are restricted and tense, lacking nuance, flexibility, colour, space. In helping them with their particular experiences of chaos, professionals help them develop a story that's more nuanced, flexible, colourful and spacious than it might otherwise be. Stern (1985) writes, 'The advent of language ultimately brings about the ability to narrate one's own life story with all the potential that holds for changing how one views oneself' (p.174).

Perhaps because he's always worked hard to keep his chaotic experience at bay, Alwyn has – by all accounts – rarely been in trouble at school until now. Now at 13 years of age, he must deal with a new man coming into his mother's life, potentially taking his place and provoking a thousand Oedipal rivalries he can't even begin to talk about. He might feel that he's been loyal and protective towards his mother during the years since his father left, only for her now to be abandoning him in favour of some new suitor. Now at 13, he's obliged to confront the dreadful realisation of his mother's sexual potential, a potential he'd rather not think about and can't satisfy as he struggles with his own pubertal conflicts. Now at 13, he's expected graciously and uncomplainingly to cede his place at his mother's side to a man who isn't even his father.

So he swears at female teachers. He refuses to do as they tell him. He insists that he wants to be expelled because he's *not* sorry for what he's done. He's forcing the school's hand ('Go on! Expel me!') as if enacting some kind of suicide, as if the only way he can kill off the conflicted feelings inside himself is to kill himself off, at least symbolically.

He might also be trying to kill off his feelings by symbolically killing off his mother, attacking female teachers in an oblique attempt to make his feelings about her go away. 'I hate my mother, but I can't bear to show her my hatred because I also love her and I don't want to become like my father,' he might be saying, if only he could speak. 'If she was also to leave me, then I'd have no one! So I take my hatred out on the mother-figures in school because they can bear it, because they won't be damaged, because they've got back-up and because they're actually not as important as my mother!' Alwyn's behaviour towards female teachers is a powerful communication that, unfortunately, makes sense, and there are plenty of perpetrators whose violence towards women makes a similarly unconscious kind of sense.

Sitting back in his chair, Alwyn's eyes flick nervously round the room, avoiding mine. When young people meet with a counsellor for the first time, their behaviour is usually an enactment of their earlier attachment experiences. In other words, they respond to the possibility of intimacy and kindness in the way that they've always responded to these things: with confidence and trust or – as in Alwyn's case – with suspicion, ever alert to the possibility of betrayal, to the possibility that any suggestion of kindness might be quickly withdrawn.

Given the story of his first five years, it would be surprising if, meeting with me, Alwyn was anything other than suspicious, even though we've already been meeting for a few weeks. Young people whose original baby-noises were of absolutely no interest to anyone will be unused to talking with any expectation of a response; they'll be reluctant to volunteer words if their words have traditionally been misunderstood or scorned or disregarded. Telling an autobiographical story involves making an attachment (Holmes 2001), a commitment to the listener, trusting that he or she will be interested and will try to understand. Alwyn's jumbled up story of the first years of his life betrays a jumbled up, chaotic experience of attachment and of himself. Things don't fit together. He doesn't fit together. So together we have to develop a story that's less jumbled up, a story without bits missing and with feelings and thoughts included (Kurtz and Coetzee 2015; Luxmoore 2017).

'I know talking's hard,' I say. 'Are you okay?'

'It's just that I don't know what to say,' he replies, wincing. 'Also, I'm not feeling very well. I'm feeling a bit sick.'

Alwyn may have the beginnings of a virus, but over the years I've worked with a surprising number of young people with phobias about sickness: about other people vomiting or about vomiting themselves. It's a phobia that stops them hanging out with friends, being in confined spaces or crowds, going on car journeys or on stage... Like all phobias, it seems to focus a more general anxiety, usually an anxiety about being uncontained, about things being out of control, about chaos erupting unexpectedly, about feelings bursting out. Alwyn may simply want to escape from our session by claiming to be sick, or he may be describing an experience of feelings bubbling inside him and a fear that they'll come pouring out.

He looks uneasy, agitated, as if something is stirring inside him. 'I really am feeling a bit sick!'

'Maybe you're sick of having to be good?' I suggest. 'Maybe you've been good and patient and quiet all these years and you've had enough?'

He stops fidgeting and looks at me, listening now.

'Maybe getting into trouble at school and telling a few people to fuck off makes sense, Alwyn?'

'Yeah, but I know I shouldn't do it,' he says. 'I know it's not the teachers' fault.'

'Like it wasn't your mum's fault...'

He's temporarily speechless, taken aback, transported – I imagine – to a time when he lost his words, when he couldn't speak; to the sound of his father beating his mother on the other side of the bedroom door.

He sighs, looking tearful. 'So why am I like this?'

'Because you've kept quiet all these years, Alwyn. Because you've always loved your mother and haven't wanted to make things worse for her. And because it's so hurtful now when she brings someone else into her life. I'm not surprised that you're feeling hurt and I'm not surprised that you're feeling angry...'

He looks relieved.

'But I don't think it's just her that you're angry with...'

He looks back at me, expecting me to tell him the answer. But he knows.

I say nothing.

Again he's speechless. Lost for words.

I wait.

He's crying a little.

'You were five years old...'

He nods, wiping away the tears. 'If I saw him now I'd kick the shit out of him! If the police had him in a cell, I'd stab the fucker to death and I wouldn't care! They could lock me up for the rest of my life – that would be fine – at least I'd know I'd done it! I'd have paid him back for what he did! I'd have smashed every fucking bone in his stupid fucking body! And if he was lying there, begging for mercy, I'd set fire to him, the fucking piece of shit!'

The words tumble out.

I've worked with many young people, usually boys, to whom bad things happened when they were too small to do anything about it. They weren't strong enough. They wanted to intervene but couldn't. They were scared. They live with the legacy of these things happening and they don't forget. They're left wanting to make up for what happened and, once they're big enough, once they're strong enough and brave enough, they look for opportunities to discharge all that rage and hatred, to rid themselves of the feelings of uselessness and failure. Sometimes, years later, they're able to do it at the expense of the original perpetrator – a father or an older brother, for example – but often the feelings get displaced onto someone who's unwittingly behaving in the same way as the original perpetrator. Except that this time it's different. This time a whole language of violence erupts to replace what – once upon a time – was speechless impotence. This time the young person feels unapologetically empowered and – however terrible the consequences – feels good, feels redeemed.

Alwyn looks calmer, having found a voice.

7

SCHOOLS AND CHAOS

A nother cold morning. The teachers and teaching assistants are back in school with classes to teach, colleagues to see, problems to solve. Six of them, who meet with me as a group for an hour every fortnight, spend the first half of this morning's session fulminating about the unfairness of being endlessly undermined by parents, of having chairs thrown at them by students, of being bitten and kicked and spat on. They want certain students excluded. They want parents held to account. They want people to realise what this work is like. They want the head teacher to sort it all out and are dismayed that she – seemingly – won't.

They explain to me how hard they're working, how much planning they're doing, how much time they spend anticipating all that could go wrong. And yet *still* there's misbehaviour, *still* there are unforeseen events, *still* there isn't enough support.

'It's just chaos!' someone says.

I have no doubt that they're working extremely hard and are by no means exaggerating the extent of the students' misbehaviour. But they work in a school for young people with extreme behavioural difficulties, and we've talked about this before. Give or take varying degrees of governmental underfunding, it feels like this every year, and every year the group dreams of a rescuer who'll arrive with The Answer, someone who'll make the chaos go away.

What's hard to accept is that we must live with a perpetual degree of chaos in our working lives: that young people are unpredictable, their moods fluctuate, they get ill, they come to school already damaged by life. And teachers themselves come to school at the same time as dealing with other things going on in their lives: with their own children misbehaving, their partners not taking responsibility, their parents becoming old and infirm.

We've got 20 minutes left before the session ends and before they must return to the chaos they describe. Someone in the group suggests contacting the Union to complain about the impossibility of the job. Someone else says that dealing with this kind of behaviour is actually part of the job.

The group thinks about this.

Someone suggests that it's the head teacher's fault for not being more involved and someone else says that the head teacher can't be all things to all people.

Again, the group pauses to think.

Someone says that because things are so bad, she's going to resign. Someone else says that we always feel like resigning when things are bad.

And so we go on: one panicky statement followed by something more placatory, the chaotic impulse temporarily contained, an anxious id assuaged by a thoughtful, hard-working ego. Our group is a microcosm of school life. In every classroom and in every staffroom there are always voices insisting that 'this school' is going downhill and that, this year, things are worse than last year (Luxmoore 2008). As far as young people are concerned, it's a voice that comes from a more general sense of life going downhill as they get older and as people demand more and more from them. 'This school' becomes a way of trying to talk about a time in their lives when things seemed simpler. It becomes a way of mourning the loss of childhood, the loss of an orderly world seemingly untouched by chaos (see Chapter 5). Young people and their parents readily project their dismay about 'this school' onto members of staff who, in turn, introject it as their own.

'I don't remember things ever being this bad,' someone comments. 'It feels like this school's losing its identity.'

We're coming towards the end of our session. Someone in the group says that there's never any substitute for good old-fashioned discipline, implying that more overt discipline would bring the chaos under control. Another member of the group quickly observes that we wouldn't want to go back to corporal punishment, however, suggesting to the group that unrelenting control might actually be as tyrannical as unrelenting chaos.

I used to be a teacher and occasionally still have dreams where my class is rioting and there's nothing I can do because I've lost control. I haven't taught for 35 years but still wake up panicky and scared. I know many teachers and ex-teachers who have exactly the same dream because the potential for situations to descend into chaos haunts us long after the danger has passed. As a teacher, you know that you must teach the curriculum in an orderly way to students who don't necessarily want to be orderly. Your mind is always aware of what could go wrong, of misbehaviour that could escalate, and once you know what it feels like to be helpless in the face of classroom chaos, the memory never leaves you.

Accepting that there will always be a degree of chaos in our lives is difficult, but until we find a way of living with our own and with other people's capacity for chaos, we struggle: the perfectionist will always be driven crazy when things don't go to plan, the workaholic will never be able to sleep, the disciplinarian will never be able to relax. Chaos reminds us unconsciously of a time before we developed a sense of our own identity and before we learned to protect that identity with adequate defence mechanisms; of a time when we were inchoate babies, fragmented, unformed and unable to defend ourselves against things spinning out of control. We've all been there and wouldn't want to go back. It's an experience buried deep in our psyches: something which, according to Winnicott (1989), 'is always at the centre of the individual, a primary chaos [or] primary state of unintegration' (p.31).

Meeting with me every week in school, there's a sense in which the group is forever presenting its chaos through the stories of its members, then trying to make sense of that chaos, trying to bear it and detoxify it.

Young people are no different. They may not sit in an organised circle of chairs on a cold morning, talking about their working lives, but they present their own oblique versions of chaos to the adults around them. They might go into a classroom and start misbehaving ostentatiously; they might approach a parent tearfully or angrily with a seemingly insoluble problem; they might meet with a counsellor and start telling stories of unfairness, aggravation, anxiety... In a sense they're forever offering up their chaos through their words or behaviours in the hope that someone – a teacher, a parent, a counsellor maybe – will be able to understand and take away the power of chaos to disturb their equilibrium.

And that's my role in the teachers' group as the outsider-facilitator-therapist: helping the group to keep thinking whenever chaos threatens to overwhelm us, whenever panic sets in and threatens to paralyse us. Mawson (1994) describes:

> ...the hope that the recipient of the projected distress might be able to bear what we cannot, and, by articulating thoughts

that we have found unthinkable, contribute to developing in us a capacity to think and to hold on to anxiety ourselves. (p.70)

However much the group might project its feelings of uselessness into me, my job is to keep thinking *about* the uselessness, trying to understand its origins and meaning, appreciating its power without being drawn into its enactment. As I indicated in the previous chapter, Bion (1963) would describe my role as that of a 'container' whose job is to listen to the presenting chaos, make sense of it, and then re-present it to the group in a way that makes better sense to them. This includes helping members of the group recognise their own capacity to be chaotic, so that when they're on the receiving end of other people's projected chaos, they can see it for what it is and not mistake it for their own. Head teachers have the same role in relation to members of staff who are upset, angry or frightened. Head teachers must listen to the stories and try to make sense of them, offering back understandings that help members of staff continue to work effectively. And head teachers hope to have someone who does the same for them (Luxmoore 2014, 2019).

Today I feel for the members of the group, living with a perpetual sense of inadequacy, doing their best when their best so rarely feels good enough. It's hard not to be overwhelmed, not to give up. But there are easier and better-paid jobs in the world than working in chaotic schools (and schools are always *potentially* chaotic), so why do teachers and teaching assistants do it? I suspect that one of the reasons why they're unconsciously drawn to the work is to deal with their own chaos. Being in a school forces us to think about our relationship with childhood and adolescence, to think about our relationship with authority and authority-figures. In effect, school forces us to live with the ever-changing relationship between order and chaos. So of course members of the group want me to be the rescuing grown-up who'll make their chaos go away. Of course they want the head teacher to wave her magic wand. Of course they'd rather not take responsibility themselves. Of course they attribute chaos to *other* people and blame *other* people for making them feel so bad.

We meet again two weeks later and nothing much has changed. Mairi says she makes lists sometimes in the middle of the night when she can't sleep. Bob reports that he goes to the gym several times a week, working on his 'core strength'. Lyra enjoys singing in a choir. Beatrice has an allotment and is doing online courses... They do these perfectly sensible things and yet *still* life in school finds ways of disrupting their equilibrium.

'It doesn't make sense!' says Kelly.

'What if the chaos never goes away?' I ask them. 'What if it's always going to be like this, give or take some ups and downs? What then? What if you work in a really dynamic place called a school where there will never be peace and tranquillity and where you probably wouldn't want peace and tranquillity even if you had it?'

Lawrence smiles and says he gets bored easily anyway.

Mairi says she longs for peace and tranquillity. She wants that more than anything else.

Beatrice says there are moments that make it worthwhile. She tells us about a boy who couldn't read when he started school but who now tells her all about the books he's reading. 'That's why I do it,' she says. 'That's what makes it worthwhile!'

In the group, hopefulness and disillusionment dance with each other all the time: the hopefulness of order (new ideas, new structures, new interventions) and the disillusionment of chaos (new things not working or not living up to our hopes for them).

Kelly says that she came into teaching because she wanted to help young people, but the curriculum is now so prescriptive that she has no time to have fun with students or to listen properly to their concerns. She says she doesn't dare to trust her own judgment and follow her instincts, for fear that she'll be criticised for not ticking the correct bureaucratic boxes. 'I'm so afraid of messing up,' she says, 'and that I'll get blamed for letting everyone down. I'm always looking over my shoulder, checking in case I've made a mess of things!'

Teachers, young people and parents refer obliquely to chaos whenever they talk about 'mess'. It's an embarrassing word and a word they use a lot: 'You're making a mess... You're so messed up... You look a mess... Your work's messy... You're messing up... Your bedroom's a total mess...' It's a word that provokes primitive anxieties in all of us, taking us back to infancy when we made messes all the time until we learned to clear up our messes and not make them in the first place. It's a word used reproachfully by people who are disposed to be kind and as an insult by people who are not. We're haunted by the messes we've made in our lives, by the ways we've messed up relationships and opportunities: precious moments now lost to us. At worst, the prospect of ever making a mess of something puts us off trying in the first place because we dread having to revisit those old feelings of humiliation and uselessness, of being incompetent, of being a child.

Inevitably, young people have strong feelings about mess, accusing others of making messes in order to deflect attention from their own capacity to mess up. For example, their anxieties about mess and messiness are implied in relation to food. Whereas babies are messy with food, spitting it out, choking on it, smearing it around, refusing to eat it or wanting more and more of it, the behaviour of young people in relation to food might usefully be understood in relation to the prospect of emotional or physical messiness, with all the dependent, infantile anxieties evoked by food.

Similarly, young people's feelings about anger, about sex, and about failure might be understood in relation to mess. So just as angry babies scream uncontrollably, making an aural mess of everything, there are some young people who fall back on their out-of-control, baby-like anger as a comforting way of relinquishing personal responsibility (see Chapter 8), while other young people are wary of ever being angry for fear of the feelings it might provoke in others.

Young people also have ambivalent feelings about the messiness of sex: some seemingly relaxed about the prospect of making any kind of mess and others panic-stricken, fastidious about keeping everything neat and tidy.

And there's another kind of mess that fills young people with anxiety: the messiness of failure. 'Failure' is a word avoided in polite educational circles, and yet young people are only too well aware of its existence and of their capacity to fail, to make a mess of things (Luxmoore 2017). Part of what makes the prospect of failure intolerable (thereby provoking all kinds of avoidant behaviours in young people) is the thought of other people's disapproval, of making a mess that can't be undone, a mess that betrays an incompetence in young people who've spent so long trying to be competent, trying to be adult, trying not to be babyish (see Chapter 5).

The way parents and parent-figures relate to the idea of 'mess' has a profound effect upon the children and young people they so want to support. Young people are always learning how much they can control their lives and how much they can't. In a sense, they're always learning how to live with mess, how to live with chaos. So what price spontaneity, with its potential for making an inappropriate mess of things? To what extent do we encourage young people ever to take risks, knowing that they might mess up? And what price playfulness? To what extent do we encourage them to try things out in everyday relationships?

To what extent do we model spontaneity and playfulness for them, confident that if we mess up it won't be the end of the world, confident that we can laugh off any embarrassment because we're happy to learn from our mistakes? At playgroup or nursery, the thought of their children taking part in 'messy play' fills many parents with horror.

Schools offer young people a story about the future that serves as a story about chaos. The story goes that the chaos of the present will be transformed by hard work and by investing in the future. Hard work will be rewarded with control and choices; hard work will deliver us from chaos. So when the promise of that orderly, happy future can't be delivered, when hard work fails to transform young people's lives, when their performance turns out to be average rather than exceptional, there's an understandable backlash from young people and from staff.

Sometimes, that backlash, that defence against chaos takes the form of increased bureaucracy, with teachers given yet more forms to fill in and students assessed only for what's quantifiable (exactly the kind of regime Kelly complains about) in the hope that this will somehow ensure the kind of future that was promised. Sometimes, the backlash tries to get rid of any potential for chaos, for things not going to plan, by re-grouping students, re-organising teachers, re-structuring the timetable, re-designating rooms: whatever it takes to ensure a future unsullied by chaos.

Meeting with me, the group defends itself in various ways against the threat of chaos: they scapegoat, they despair, they deny their feelings. Typically, chaos comes to be represented by a particular student who *hasn't* been transformed despite everyone's hard work and forbearance. This archetypal student's name changes from year to year as different students emerge and hold the role for a while before moving on and being replaced in the collective unconscious of the group. Members of the group describe the abusiveness of the student's upbringing, the hopelessness of his parents, the way he refuses all attempts to save himself, as if he's wilfully embracing chaos. His behaviour confounds and upsets the group because it suggests that the prevailing school story isn't enough, that chaos will sometimes triumph over order and that their efforts will sometimes be in vain.

As they talk vehemently about him, they're pulled in different directions. There's a part of them that wants to rescue him from himself, and another part of them that wants to persecute him, to teach him a lesson that he'll never forget. In a sense, they love and they hate him. He represents all their hopefulness and all their despair, their own internal chaos as well as that of the wider world. In other words, it's personal. Very personal. And although these are hard things to think about, again and again we come back to the very mixed feelings we have about students. This is important for the group to do because, as Jersild (1955) writes about teachers and teaching, 'The more courage and humility we can bring to bear in facing our hostility, the less destructive it is likely to be' (p.117).

'What happens to your own chaos,' I ask, looking round. 'To the parts of you that can be messy and a bit mad?'

Kelly starts talking about her week and cries. She never misses a day of school, she says. She wouldn't dream of letting down her colleagues or her students, and yet she dreads coming to work at the moment, knowing what each day will be like.

Mairi doesn't cry, but admits to similar feelings of dread, afraid that her situation will never change and that these feelings will go on for ever: unhappy, unsupported, unable to relax or sleep.

It takes courage to go to work when we're scared of what might happen, when we're feeling bullied and know that the day ahead will be tense with unpredictable, hurtful events bound to happen. Good teaching depends on maintaining good relationships, but maintaining those relationships takes courage when the people around us can be so belligerent and vindictive.

I say this to the group, adding, 'You might feel like lashing out yourselves sometimes...'

And suddenly they're off, with stories about what they've *felt* like saying, *felt* like doing: laughing, recognising each other's predicaments, knowing what it feels like to be confronted by an abusive parent or an unsympathetic colleague or an out-of-control student.

'I've written my resignation letter so many times!' says Kelly.

The others admit that they, too, have written resignation letters, at least in their heads.

They're smiling and the mood has lifted. I tell them that I think their courage is impressive; that it'll win no prizes, no pay rises or public recognition, and yet it'll be what holds so many young people together and makes a difference in their lives. 'That's what courage is,' I remind them, 'when we feel afraid, but do it anyway. When we do it because it matters. Because young people's lives matter.'

I have a terrible sense of hopelessness, of my fine words being all very well but changing nothing because the human potential for chaos never goes away. If the students at the school are lucky, though, courageous teachers like Mairi, Kelly, Bob, Lyra, Lawrence and Beatrice won't be going away either. And my job, I know, isn't ultimately to come up with fine words, but to survive, bearing the chaos with them and – in so doing – helping them also to survive.

8

ANGER, SHAME AND CHAOS

James is furious. 'None of it's true!' he says. 'To be honest, I can't remember that much, because one minute we were in the kitchen talking, and the next we were outside getting fresh air. I'd definitely had a few drinks. And I admit I liked her, but she didn't seem that interested, so I wasn't expecting anything. We might have had a kiss, but nothing more. Definitely none of the stuff she's saying! No way!'

I ask what she is saying.

'She's saying we were down at the end of the garden, away from the others, and she reckons I fingered her and then tried to have sex with her. Tried to force myself on her. Which I definitely didn't do! I mean, I was pissed – I admit that – but I wasn't *that* pissed, and anyway I'd never do that to a girl. Not if she didn't want to. I'm just not that kind of person...' He looks frightened. 'You can ask anyone!'

Some young people respond to chaos by trying to control everything while others despair, run away, get drunk, get high... Still others get angry: angry that everything seems to be going wrong, that they keep making mistakes, that other people don't understand, that the world is frustrating and that nothing is ever as good as it's supposed to be. Freud (1914a) proposes the idea of an 'ego ideal', perhaps internalised from our originally 'ideal' mothers: a sense of how we could be, if only... If only we weren't so *stupid*! If only we weren't so *disorganised*! If only we weren't such a *mess*!

'If only everything wasn't falling apart!' James might add. 'And if only my whole life hadn't been ruined!'

In the same way that Winnicott (1986) describes panic attacks as 'anxiety that can't be thought about', young people's angry outbursts might be described as chaos that can't be thought about. For some, anger is an expression of chaos, a lashing-out, a description of something out of control and impossible to think about. But for others, anger is a *defence* against chaos, an attempt to shoehorn the sprawling disruption of chaos into a single manageable behaviour. James seems intent on his anger, presumably as a defence against feeling afraid or ashamed or responsible for what did or didn't happen with Alice. I imagine he's deploying his anger now as a way of holding himself together, as a way of staying in control and scaring people off.

'No one's talking to me! All her mates are going round saying I'm a rapist! And the boys – including the ones who were supposed to be my mates – are all siding with her, sucking up to her like none of them have ever done anything wrong in their fucking lives! And I wouldn't give a toss, except that what she's saying isn't true. I never did anything, I swear on my life! And now they're talking about getting the police involved. And the school's phoned my parents, so they know all about it, and apparently her parents might be wanting to press charges or something...'

Some young people respond to shame by trying to deflect it onto someone else ('It wasn't me! It was you!'), while others respond by telling lies ('I didn't do it, honestly!'), holding on to those lies for all they're worth. I have absolutely no idea whether or not James is telling the truth. I could ask, but at this stage he'd feel obliged to maintain the story he's just been telling me. There's certainly a huge discrepancy between his story ('We might have had a kiss') and Alice's story that he tried to rape her. I suspect that James isn't telling me everything.

Shame is a particularly dreadful kind of chaos, stripping away our defences and leaving us with nowhere to hide. In addition to the shame currently being heaped on him by his peers, I imagine that James will also feel ashamed because he'll have *imagined* having impromptu sex with girls, and so his denials might not feel as convincing as he'd like them to feel.

'They're calling me a rapist and I'm not! I never did anything!'

I imagine the self-righteousness of the other boys, using James's story to distance themselves from anything so despicable as rape. And I imagine Alice's friends, loyal to their friend, upset and shocked by what's happened, but also excited to be so close to such an important story. I wonder to myself whether asking James to describe in detail exactly what happened in the garden would help as a way of getting the real story out into the open, 'Was she wearing jeans or a skirt, James? Where were your hands? Exactly what did you do?'

Somehow I have to get him thinking again because shame paralyses and stops us thinking, locking us into defensive behaviours as we struggle to survive. Kohut (1971) describes the way we develop a sense of ourselves out of the relationships we internalise as we grow up ('This is who I am') but that we live in fear of these fledgling selves fragmenting and being crushed. We're forever alert to any potential threat. So James has got his indignation, his anger, his story, and he's holding on to these things for dear life, as if they're all he's got. He's no longer able to improvise, no longer able to think, intent only on saving face. He may well have made a terrible mistake, drunkenly believing that he could behave as he chose with Alice regardless of her feelings and regardless of her consent. If that's true, he'll deserve some kind of punishment and she'll certainly deserve everyone's support. But young people do make sexual mistakes and, unless there are criminal proceedings, shame is typically their punishment: the shame of sexual rejection, the shame they must bear if the relationship is to continue, or the public kind of shame that James is experiencing.

'They've been calling me a rapist and a pervert! One of her friends wrote that I'm an animal! They're calling me a paedophile!'

He's 16. Alice is a year younger. When young people are shamed in public like this, they become dangerous, capable of lashing out at other people or at themselves when the shame feels impossible to bear, when it feels as if their sense of themselves is being crushed. Sometimes they kill themselves as a way of killing the shame (Murphy 2017). So I have to help James manage the shame and the chaos enveloping him. Somehow I have to get him thinking again before he makes a bad situation worse.

With many young people, the therapeutic task is to find the anger that's hidden away, repressed or displaced into other behaviours, because without their anger young people lose their energy and passion and become depressed. They need their anger to animate their lives (Luxmoore 2006). But with James, the task seems to be the other way round: he appears to be using anger as a defence, as a way of trying to deflect attention away from the shame he's feeling inside, from the humiliation he's experiencing, from the threat to his reputation and whole sense of himself. I have to help him find a way out of this impasse, out of this angry, high-stakes, all-or-nothing, my-word-against-her-word war that he's fighting. Otherwise, something will break.

It would be of no comfort whatsoever to Alice, but it could be that James was trying to be affectionate, to be close to her, perhaps in the only way he knew. It could be that he was behaving as he'd seen his father behave towards women or as he'd seen men behaving in pornography. Perhaps his behaviour was an expression of anxiety rather than spite?

'You said you liked her, James…?'

He looks surprised. 'I didn't mean I liked her for sex,' he says defensively. 'I meant I liked her as a friend. She was good to talk to. And I thought we were getting on okay.'

'You might have been feeling close to her? Fond of her…?'

'I suppose so,' he says, abashed. 'I definitely liked her. Which is why I'm pissed off now that she's saying all this, because I would never do anything to hurt her!'

'Maybe you felt close to her and wanted to take the relationship further?'

'Yeah,' he says, 'but not if she didn't want to.'

'Maybe you loved her?'

He thinks about this. 'I suppose, in a way… But that's all fucked up now, isn't it! She's already told everyone that she's never going to speak to me again! And I wouldn't blame her if any of it was true, but it's not!'

Chaos has come crashing down on him. James finds himself disbelieved, ostracised, shamed. But the mess of chaos is harder to assimilate if we remain inflexible, unable to improvise and unable to acknowledge the chaotic parts of ourselves. James is insisting that his story is all there is to know, that it's his word against Alice's. He might cope better and eventually feel less ashamed if he's able to develop a more flexible story about himself as someone (like other people) capable of making mistakes, of getting carried away, of being stupidly lustful and behaving terribly sometimes, because at the moment, as Freud (1912) has it, 'he is in danger of never finding anything but what he already knows' (p.112).

I'm not proposing to help him make up some story that avoids having to take personal responsibility for what happened. Rather, this is about helping him to understand himself a little better because he's well and truly stuck. He's admitted that he was drunk. With that in mind, he might usefully add some uncertainty and some remorse to his story, some acknowledgement that he might not be entirely sure about what happened, because for now he's effectively saying to himself, 'If I keep repeating the same story, I'll be able to control the story rather than be controlled by the story.' As a strategy, it's not working. Before long, he'll lose any last remaining friends and, in my experience, be obliged to move schools and start all over again somewhere else. Or something worse could happen. Sometimes young people try to kill themselves as the only way out of a trap.

'You might not have meant to do anything wrong, but maybe you made a mistake, James?'

'Are you saying that I'm lying?'

'No, I'm not saying that you're lying. I'm saying that everyone has their own truths. You might have thought you were being cool, but Alice might have thought you were taking advantage. You might not have meant it to come across like that, but she might not have known what to do or say to stop you. She might have felt like she was about to be raped... Even if you didn't mean it like that.'

There's always a context. I've known James for a while and know that his life has always been chaotic. He's moved back and forth between his parents' houses: between his mother complaining that she can't cope with him any more and his father insisting on house rules more suitable for a toddler than a teenager. Like many parents, they seem to have expected that 'rules' alone would deal with the chaos of family and adolescent life. Over the years they've broken their own rules and then got mad when James has also gone and broken them.

'You said the school's already phoned your parents... What will they say, James?'

'Probably nothing,' he mumbles, distracted. 'They'll have a go at me in front of the teachers like they always do, but they won't really care as long as it doesn't affect them. Whenever I get into trouble, they're only interested in what other people are going to think about them.'

I'm reminded of the shame parents feel when their child is guilty of some misdemeanour. With the self-righteous world looking on, parents are inclined to lash out in the same way that young people lash out, either at their child ('You're no fucking son of mine!'), or at the authorities involved ('Who the fuck are you to accuse my son!'), or at the sneering bystanders ('Don't think you're so fucking perfect yourselves!'). The shame of being thought of as a bad parent is terrible.

James is lashing out, full of affronted anger in response to the shame he's experiencing. Mollon (2002) describes this kind of anger as deriving 'from childhood experiences of humiliation and [from] failures to evoke empathic understanding from care-givers' (p.46). It's as if James assumes no one will understand him, no one will take his side; he must fight alone as he's always fought alone, responding to this situation as he's always responded to chaotic situations in his life in the absence of any parental support.

This may be unfair on his parents. But secure attachments – knowing that we matter to other people and can rely on them – help us to regulate our internal chaos and the external chaos we encounter in life (Holmes 2001). With secure attachments we know that – under pressure – we're never alone, that we can survive chaos because people love us and will be waiting for us once the chaos has subsided. My understanding from our earlier work together is that James never did feel securely attached in his formative relationships. He always felt alone, always felt unworthy. Lacking *internal* confidence in himself, he's always searched for *external* ways of dealing with chaos. When he felt miserable or unloved, he got drunk or got stoned; when he felt afraid, he ran away from situations. His current behaviour – clinging to anger as a way of keeping himself safe while insisting that he's right and that Alice is wrong – is simply his best attempt to manage the situation.

Shame is a familiar, abiding experience for many young people. Cozolino (2016) identifies what he calls 'core shame' as the shame of not feeling loved. He traces it back to our first experiences with a mother or care-giver and to our sense of being unlovable when that person turns her back or refuses our requests or seems more interested in other people. 'I'm not good enough... I can't be sure that she loves me... I must keep control of her or she'll leave me...' James's behaviour with Alice might have been informed not only by lust but also by a deeper fear that unless he held on to her tightly, he'd inevitably lose her. In other words, his sexual behaviour might have been the expression of attachment anxiety and might have been – iron-ically – an attempt to *avoid* being shamed. This isn't for one moment to excuse the behaviour, but merely an attempt to understand it. If I can help him to understand himself better, he might be able to live less impulsively, thinking more clearly and exercising more choice in his life.

I repeat, 'She might have felt like she was about to be raped, James. Even if you didn't mean it like that.'

He thinks about this, wondering where this leaves his story and whether he can afford to acknowledge the possibility of what I'm suggesting without losing face.

'Other people haven't always understood you, James...'

He looks confused. 'What d'you mean?'

'I mean that in the past other people have sometimes thought you were being controlling or mean to them when actually you were wanting to be close to them. Like all of us, you're a person who needs to feel close to other people – to trust them, to be able to rely on them – and in the past that's meant that you've sometimes tried too hard and other people haven't liked it.'

He's listening.

I decide to put my cards on the table. 'What happened with Alice might have been a mistake: a bad mistake, and one that you'll probably need to admit and apologise for. But people will need to understand that making a mistake doesn't make you a bad person, just a person who needs to feel close to people and gets scared when he thinks he might be losing them.'

He's still listening, still giving me the benefit of the doubt.

'And you're also a person who gets horny sometimes, which you need to deal with in the future without ever, *ever* hurting anyone!'

We both smile. He knows that I like him and that I know there's more to him than meets the eye. I imagine he's pleased that I know this because it's a relief for young people not to be taken at face value. However, the stakes are very high at the moment because he's insisting on his story, giving himself no room for manoeuvre. Chaos is never conquered: we just find better ways of living with it. I'm suggesting a less rigid, more conciliatory, less all-or-nothing story: a way of trying to live with the chaos that's erupted in his life rather than trying to fight it.

Young people go to see counsellors and other professionals when the ways they're dealing with life aren't working. Usually the young people have become too rigid in their thinking or in their behaviour. Their defence mechanisms are out of date. The therapeutic task is therefore to help them develop more flexible strategies, more nuanced, up-to-date autobiographies, more imaginative ways of thinking about the world. But daring to look with a counsellor at what might be behind their habitual defence mechanisms means that the threat of shame is constant. Big, scary, angry James might be exposed as someone secretly needing to be loved. So if I've mistimed what I've just said to him, if our relationship isn't strong enough yet to cope with such a robust suggestion, the danger is that he'll feel exposed and shamed: he'll pick up his anger and storm out of the room, telling me to go and fuck myself.

He hasn't stormed out. He looks as if he's twisting himself into knots, though, thinking through what I've just said about the need to apologise. Wieland-Burston (1992) writes about chaos, 'What counts in the long run is not that we stand and face the monster, but that we realize and can admit to ourselves that we are afraid and would like to flee' (p.136).

'So what am I supposed to do?' he asks, looking up.

'You could go round to her house...?'

'No way! Her dad would kill me!'

'You could phone first and ask if you could come round...'

'What if her parents are there?'

'They will be!'

'And what if they say, no, don't even dare to come round?'

He's right to be scared, not only about the possibility of being beaten up by Alice's family, but also about having to confront what's happened and of having to apologise for his behaviour. The alternative would be to stick with his denial that anything happened between himself and Alice, a story no one believes.

'You'll have to accept that you've lost your friendship with her, James. Things won't go back to how they were. But this is about repairing some of the damage and not pretending. And whatever you do to make things better, it'll take a lot of guts...'

There's a longer-term issue for James and, I'm sure, for Alice as well who's had a horrible experience. Some young people never fully recover when relationships end suddenly. Terrible things are said at the time, while other things are left unsaid which lie hidden for years as unexploded bombs. Always there's anger and shame. And there can be a lifelong legacy of avoiding intimacy, of never committing to relationships because the original hurt has never really gone away.

'It's important to apologise when we've made a mistake,' I say to him, 'even if it feels as if no one in our lives ever apologises to us. Because once we've apologised and meant it, we can sleep at night. If we haven't apologised, there's always this thing, nagging away, telling us that we're bad. And you're not a bad person, James. You're a good person. But you've probably made a bad mistake.'

He looks scared. 'Oh, fuck!' he says. Then, after thinking about it some more, '*Oh, fuck!*'

9
JOYLESSNESS AND CHAOS

David's miserable. And after a few sessions I discover that he's *always* miserable. I see his name in my diary in the morning and think to myself, 'Oh no, I've got David Buckland today!', imagining another cheerless session full of gloom and doom.

I try to greet him with enthusiasm. I try to have a few topics up my sleeve for when our conversation inevitably flags. Sometimes I share with him a few quirky or irreverent bits of information about myself in the hope that he'll reciprocate. But no. There's no spark. He doesn't smile. Instead, I'm dragged back into the slough of despond, the apparent joylessness of his life.

'So why?' I ask myself. 'Why's he like this? Why does he do this to me? Why can't I ever look forward to seeing him? Has something happened to him in the past or is he just *like this*?'

I could ask. I could say, 'David, nothing ever seems to go well in your life. You seem completely joyless. You're never happy and you never seem to take pleasure in anything... Has it always felt like this? Has something happened to take away your happiness?'

During a Quidditch match, Harry Potter is hospitalised after being attacked by the Dementors. Professor Lupin warns him,

'Get too near a Dementor and every good feeling, every happy memory will be sucked out of you' (Rowling 1999, p.140). Poor David! Although there are people in the world who – like the Dementors – seem determined to kill off the joy in others, his effect on me isn't remotely that bad. Yet for those of us who like to think of ourselves as reasonably joyful people, the joylessness of others can be disconcerting. The assumption behind most counselling and psychotherapy is that people want to be happy, or at least happier, to be more joyful, otherwise they wouldn't be bothering to talk to a therapist. So does David want more joy in his life? Or is he perfectly content with things as they are? He functions normally: sleeping well, always getting out of bed in the mornings, eating properly, walking to school, concentrating well enough in lessons, interacting with his peers... He's not clinically depressed. He's not autistic. There's just a joylessness about him.

'It's really nice to see you, David,' I say, greeting him with my biggest smile. 'How's your week been?'

'Okay,' he replies dolefully. 'Nothing special.'

'What would "special" be like?'

He looks confused.

'I mean, what would make your week exciting or fun or really worthwhile?'

'Nothing really,' he says. 'It was an okay week.'

'What happened?'

'Nothing much.'

'Anything really good or really bad?'

He looks back at me, unmoved. 'Not really.'

I think to myself... If joyfulness is partly about spontaneity and the chaos of spontaneity, about delighting in things that happen quite suddenly, then joyless people might be afraid of spontaneity for historical reasons: because for them spontaneity is associated with sudden violence, or with sexual aggression, or with things being out of control, with shame, with that kind of chaos. As a response to the world, joylessness would make sense, therefore, as a way of keeping everything under control, under scrutiny, as a way of trying to ensure that nothing untoward happens.

But I can find nothing in David's story that might obviously have damaged him in these ways. With apparent candour, he recounts the circumstances of his 16-year-old life and it sounds relatively uneventful. No abusive parents. No conspicuous bullying. No sudden events taking his life in unforeseen directions. I try and fail to rouse any anger in him, to find any sense of life being unfair. So why is he coming to see me? He's uninterested in romance, in friendships, in music, in sport. He seems to regard school as he regards life: as a succession of opportunities to be endured rather than seized.

I wonder to myself whether his joylessness serves as an attachment object: whether David limits himself to certain predictable experiences and behaviours, because that way he stays safe and knows where he stands? I wonder about the Lacanian idea of *jouissance* (Fink 1997), about people who get pleasure from pain, or satisfaction from dissatisfaction; about people who come to therapy because their symptoms are under some sort of threat and they look to therapy to shore up or maintain these symptoms, not to make them go away. Perhaps David enjoys being miserable? Perhaps he's afraid of pleasure, of things going well and of what that might entail?

'I know you were dreading it, David, but you got a really good mark in your test... Well done!'

He acknowledges what I've said, but no smile.

'And it must have felt good getting your job fixed up for the summer holidays?'

Nothing.

When we first started meeting, my understanding was that he wanted to 'talk over some stuff' with me. So we talked about his life – about people, about school, about his choice of academic subjects for next year. Nothing stood out. But to my surprise he was clear at the end of the session that he wanted to meet again and to keep meeting. Our session had been – he said in his most deadpan way – helpful.

William Carlos Williams's famously short poem 'The Red Wheelbarrow' (1976) is about the importance of noticing things that appear mundane. So much depends on doing that. Echoing Williams, Phillips (2019) begins a book by insisting that 'Everything depends on what, if anything, we find interesting...' (p.3). I agree with both of them. The job of a therapist is to be interested in the client, however mundane the client's material, in order to interest the client in himself so that he wants to know more, to discover what's hidden, to look at himself from different angles, to develop a wider repertoire of responses to the world and, in so doing, feel more confident, more at ease. This is an extension of the job of a parent or carer: being interested and remaining interested in the baby so that the baby eventually learns to be interested in itself and in its surroundings, no longer encased in a narcissistic cocoon but confident of itself in relation to other people, able to interact with them without fear of being boring or invisible. Perhaps David's parents were never particularly interested in their only child? Perhaps his joylessness is a kind of identification with them or loyalty to them (Schafer 2003)? Alvarez (1992) writes that parents need to be 'alerters, arousers and enliveners of their babies' (p.60), otherwise babies lose interest in the world and become depressed. Part of my job, I tell myself, is therefore to remain interested in David, however much he appears to make himself deliberately uninteresting. I have to try – somehow – to be an enlivening presence, instilling some degree of joyfulness into this seemingly joyless young person. Alvarez argues elsewhere (2012) that we learn not only through our experience of frustration but also through our experience of satisfaction, through the experience of other people delighting us and being delighted in us. She warns (1992), however, that

> [t]his type of cheering up needs to be distinguished from the kind of manic reassurance and denial of depression which could encourage the development of a 'false self' in a child who, for example, has to cheer himself up in order to cheer his mother up. (p.61)

So my delighting in David mustn't be gushing or desperate.

He may not be interested in the conventions of adolescence – romance, friendship, music, sport – but David does have interests. He likes playing chess, he tells me, and we spend most of one session with him patiently teaching me the rules, talking me through my mistakes, helping me to improve. He plays chess with his grandfather, he says, but rarely sees his grandfather who lives far away. When I ask about the possibility of starting a chess club at school, he says he's too busy with schoolwork. When I ask whether the responsibility of setting up and running something like that would be scary, he says no, it just wouldn't be his thing.

He reveals that he's also interested in old, black-and-white films.

I ask what it is about these films that he particularly enjoys.

'I just like them,' he says, blankly.

When I enthuse about the black-and-white westerns I remember from childhood, he acknowledges my enthusiasm but doesn't reciprocate.

I ask if he's seen *Shane* with Alan Ladd. 'If that was me, I'd never have Shane's patience,' I tell him. 'I'd want to shoot all the baddies!'

David tells me that the point of the film is not to use violence unless you have to.

'But David, don't you ever want to let rip? To let go of your frustrations? To take revenge on the people who've been mean to you?'

He shakes his head. 'No one's ever really been mean to me.'

I wonder whether the fact of these films being in black-and-white has some meaning for David. A chessboard is also black-and-white.

'Would it make a difference if the films were in colour?'

'They're not.'

'But if they were...?'

'I'd have to see them first, to make up my mind,' he says, not unreasonably.

Suddenly the door of our room bursts open.

'Sorry!' blurts an excited younger boy, probably escaping from someone. 'Sorry! I didn't realise!' He dashes out again and the door closes.

David has shrunk into his chair, cowed and pale.

I apologise for the interruption.

He assures me that it's okay.

If joyfulness involves investing in life ('*joie de vivre*') despite knowing life's potential for disappointment and chaos, David's joylessness might be understood as an extreme kind of cautiousness. There are parents whose fears about what could go wrong in any situation cause them to shield their children from life, instilling in them such an awareness of the potential dangers all around that their children are effectively disabled, never daring to try new things, restricting themselves only to what they know already and have already practised. Laughter is usually rare, perhaps because jokes – in a sense – are always about chaos of one sort or another (Freud 1905): about things that don't fit together, about misunderstandings, double-meanings, incongruities, chaotic ideas to be avoided at all costs.

Some young people enjoy the catharsis of laughter, relishing their ability to appreciate things that don't make obvious sense, confident that the chaos described implicitly in the joke doesn't trouble them. David never laughs. He's always punctual, though, and always polite, always deferential. I discover that he's interested in politics, one of the subjects he plans to study in the future. We talk about some of the country's recent political goings-on, about which he's extremely well-informed. A famous politician has just been caught cheating on his wife.

I ask what David thinks about this.

'Depends on whether it's in the public interest,' he says. 'We don't know if it's affecting his work, or if he's given away any secrets. He's said a lot in the past about the importance of marriage, so maybe he's being a hypocrite...'

I'm impressed. I make a joke about men not being able to keep their trousers on.

He thinks about this. 'It's always happened, though,' he says, sounding like a middle-aged professor, keen to put a lid on anything potentially chaotic. 'People have always done it and politicians are no different from anyone else. In the past there have been kings and queens...'

'So are you saying that this kind of behaviour is inevitable?'

As usual, he thinks before answering. 'It's not for me to say. Obviously I've never been married or anything like that, so I wouldn't know.'

'Would you like to be married, David?'

He looks back at me calmly. 'Not really.'

It would be easy to start pushing our conversation towards subjects like sex and power and betrayal, trying to find the conflicts in David, his personal animosities and longings, his strongest and most problematic feelings. Surely there's a spark buried inside him? But I think I have to accept that not everyone wants or needs to be conventionally 'happy' or 'sad'. I may be inclined to think of David as miserable, pessimistic and joyless; I may experience him as emotionally withholding in our relationship. But unlike Molière's *misanthrope*, there's no self-righteousness in him, no moral superiority. Whereas most young people are absolutely sure that the real problem in their lives is other people, David seems perfectly happy for other people to be the way they are. He doesn't complain about them. He simply has his own satisfactions, which are different from theirs. It would be easy for him to avoid me and have nothing to do with counselling. But I think he probably comes to see me because he's worried that, at some level, his satisfactions – chess, black-and-white films, politics – aren't good enough, and he wants to be good enough, to do the right thing. 'Should I be different,' he might be asking, implicitly, 'or am I okay as I am? Everyone else seems to be up and down; everyone else is always excited or laughing or crying... Should I be more like that?'

And I realise, of course, that my answer would be, 'No, you're fine as you are, David.'

I might think but *not* say to him, 'Actually, you're an enigma, David! But the fact that you're evidently getting something from our conversations is fine, even if I don't wholly understand what it is that you're getting. Perhaps my need to feel useful, my therapist's need to understand and my uneasiness about not understanding, about the unknown, are the real problems here!'

10

CONTAINMENT AND CHAOS

As I've been describing throughout this book, young people are helped when their chaos is recognised and contained. Not denied, not repressed, not displaced, but contained in a way that prevents the chaos becoming destructive and allows it to become a potentially creative force in the young person's life. Adults help this process when they understand and acknowledge the inevitability of chaos, 'Of course bad things will sometimes happen to you... Of course you'll sometimes mess things up... Of course you'll feel like giving up...'

Conversations between young people and professionals – especially counselling conversations – can sometimes seem amorphous and unstructured: the implication being that young people will necessarily find their own truths within themselves. Sometimes this freewheeling experience makes things worse rather than better for the young person, activating the very internal chaos that he or she was hoping to contain. It takes a lot of self-assurance for young people to cope with prolonged silences or with seemingly unstructured conversations. The danger is that they walk out ('This is pointless!'), find an excuse to leave early ('I've just remembered that I'm supposed to be meeting my mum!') or simply don't come back ('I'm okay now. I don't think I need to come any more...').

Of course, it's sometimes appropriate for a counsellor to say very little, if that frees a silenced young person to find his or her voice, or if it jolts a young person into taking more responsibility for the conversation. But more often than not, a lack of structure is unhelpful in my experience, with some counsellors reluctant to play their part in structuring conversations or in ever saying what they think for fear of seeming overbearing or judgmental. By concentrating only on creating a supportive environment and never daring to say anything incisive, counsellors can never be accused of making a 'mistake'. But they *need* to make mistakes. The best therapeutic relationships will always include ruptures: moments or periods of misunderstanding, of mis-attunement between the counsellor and young person, which can then be repaired over time. Young people need this experience of rupture and repair, of temporary interpersonal chaos turning into something productive, in order for them to learn to bear misfortune, trusting that relationships won't remain stuck for ever but will eventually find ways forward.

Rigorous professionals endlessly debate these dilemmas... How directive or non-directive to be? How best to be containing without being constraining? I want to describe one particularly undervalued kind of containment...

As I mentioned in Chapter 3, I went to a strange boarding school where mixed in with the dreadful teachers were others who were kind, supportive and intellectually curious. Late one night, aged 16, I managed to entrap one of them in my study on the pretext of asking about an essay I was writing. I'd never talked to anyone about the personal stuff that was bugging me at the time, so I was circumspect, wary of how he might react, hoping that he'd guess at stuff I wasn't necessarily telling but needed him to understand nonetheless.

He listened. He asked a few questions. He let me talk. All of which was fine except that I wanted more. I didn't want to be told what to do, but nor did I just want attentive, careful listening. I wanted some perspective, some way of contextualising my experience. He was, after all, someone I admired, someone older and more experienced, someone who'd probably been through similar experiences and who, I imagined, would have drawn his own conclusions along the way. I knew that I didn't necessarily have to share those conclusions but I wanted to know what they were.

I didn't ask and he didn't say. Had I asked, he'd probably have deflected my question like a good listener, keen for me to come to my own conclusions, keen for me to develop my own understandings of the world.

He was undoubtedly a good listener. He gave me space. He didn't interrupt and didn't embarrass me. He helped me find words for some of the things I was struggling to say and, by not asking, respected the things I didn't want to say... *But I wanted more!*

Now, 47 years later, I'm running a training day for counsellors who work with young people, and it's time for us to turn our earlier theorising into practice. One of the counsellors has volunteered to be a young person arriving for a first session. Another has volunteered, somewhat reluctantly, to be herself in the role of counsellor.

Relieved that the two of them have volunteered, the rest of us watch from the safety of the audience as the counsellor and young person begin to talk.

The counsellor is trying her best, paying close attention to everything that the young person is saying, and doing what

I imagine she's been taught to do: reflecting the (imaginary) young person back to himself, scrupulously keeping herself out of the equation in order to allow the young person to explore things for himself. And yet he's clearly not getting something from the counsellor. Their conversation flags, becomes more stilted. The energy level drops.

Before long, things get stuck. I intervene and ask the counsellor what she thinks is happening.

'I don't know,' she says. 'I don't really know where to go with this...'

Members of the audience suggest possibilities. Some of them think that the counsellor could be giving a little more of herself.

'I know,' says the counsellor, 'but we've been taught to keep ourselves out of it.'

I suggest to her that most young people – indeed, most *people* – are looking for a relationship, for a connection, for some kind of exchange when they go to see a counsellor. They want their counsellor to be as real as possible.

She looks alarmed. 'I can hear my tutors telling me not to do that, though,' she says. 'It might be what I want to do, but we've been taught to let the client do the talking.'

I say that I doubt whether her tutors intended their trainees never to connect or interact, never to dare to have a point of view. They were probably just warning against counsellors taking over the conversation and this advice might have been heard by some trainees as 'I mustn't say anything about myself for fear of saying everything about myself!'

I ask what she happens to be thinking about the young person sitting opposite.

She shares with us her perfectly sensible, perceptive insights into the boy's situation. 'But I couldn't say any of that,' she says, 'because that would be imposing what I think.'

We ask the boy, still in role, how he'd feel about the counsellor saying some of what she's been thinking.

'It's actually what I want,' he says. 'I'm beginning to run out of things to say and I've got no idea if I'm making any sense, going on and on about my parents. And,' he says, turning to the counsellor, 'what you just said makes total sense, so I wish you'd go ahead and say it!'

I think there are times when it's necessary for counsellors to offer their wisdom for the benefit of the other person. I don't mean mindlessly dishing out advice without listening to the other person, nor do I mean offering mirroring statements that simply give back to the other person variations on whatever he or she has already been saying perfectly well. Occasionally there's a place for advice, if, having thought about it, the counsellor decides that it's really what the client most needs at that moment. And often there's a need for mirroring that assures the client that he or she does make sense and is understandable, at least to the counsellor.

What I mean by 'wisdom' is neither of these things. What I mean is a slightly detached perspective based on the counsellor's own learning from life that's relevant to what the other person has been talking about. It's a perspective often prefaced by the phrase 'In my experience...' It's a perspective that a teacher might share with a 16-year-old at boarding school: 'In my experience, it's really difficult when our love for someone isn't reciprocated, and often there's nothing we can do but wait and hope and accept that it might never be reciprocated...' It's a perspective that a counsellor might share with a role-playing boy struggling to make sense of his parents: 'In my experience, people are often disappointing,' the counsellor might say. 'They're never as bad as we fear, but nor are they usually as wonderful as we want them to be...' It's a perspective never offered as any sort of conclusion or solution to a problem and never offered as an alternative to letting a young person talk.

Nor is it a judgment, although I think it's important for counsellors sometimes to say what they're thinking. I've written elsewhere (Luxmoore 2017) about the myth of the non-judgmental counsellor because I agree with Nina Coltart's observation (Molino 1997) that '[w]hatever [counsellors] say about being non-judgmental, or about being neutral on matters of morality is, of course, absolute bunkum' (p.203). The theoretical biases of therapists are usually rooted in their own life experiences. Like anyone, they can't help but propound ideas that make sense to them in the light of those experiences, in the way that my own boarding school experience partly informs this chapter. At some level, all theorists are writing autobiographical stories, trying to generalise from their accumulated life experience for the benefit of other people, because without that life experience, they'd have nothing to say.

I suspect that many counsellors (like the well-meaning counsellor on my training day) try hard to remain neutral or 'non-judgmental', shutting out their own life experiences and ending up sounding a bit lifeless. At worst, they sound weird, repeating things that have already been said, summarising and then summarising some more. I think the idea of counsellors being 'non-judgmental' is simplistic. Of course we don't need a counsellor to make us feel worse about ourselves and we don't need to be told what to do or think, but there are times when we need a perspective, a steer, a way of thinking about our lives and gauging how they compare with other people's. We need our counsellors to be experienced people – not innocents, not people who've led sheltered lives – and sometimes we need the benefit of our counsellors' experience.

I'm not suggesting that wise counsellors therefore need to be old counsellors. One of the very best counsellors I know began seeing people in her early twenties and was already very skilled at that relatively young age. Younger counsellors might feel less confident about sharing whatever they've learned from life, but they do have their own experience and – potentially – that experience is just as therapeutically helpful for a young person as the experience of someone much older. What matters is that we consider our experience before presenting it to other people. 'Who am I about to say this *for*?' we might ask ourselves. 'Is it to satisfy myself in some way or because I judge that it's what this young person most needs right now in order to develop some perspective?'

Aristotle uses the word 'phronesis' to describe the practical kind of wisdom I'm describing: not technical wisdom (the ability to fix car engines) and not intellectual wisdom (the ability to understand black holes), but a worldly understanding born of reflection and experience. With hindsight, I wish I'd interrupted my training session with the counsellors and asked each of them to think about these questions: 'What practical wisdom have you learned in your life? How might that learning be useful to other people in counselling? And if you judged that your learning was likely to be useful, how would you go about offering it to someone?'

Nowadays I find myself saying things to young people like, 'In my experience, hating the people we love is normal... In my experience, when someone dies or leaves us – even when it's not their fault – there's usually a part of us that's angry with them... In my experience, life is usually a mixture of good and bad experiences, so beware of people pretending that everything's bound to turn out for the best... In my experience, it's useful to have a plan but important to be able to change the plan if it's not working... In my experience, it can be hard to know what we mean by love... In my experience, we sometimes focus on the little things in order not to think about the big things... In my experience, there'll always be parts of our lives that are chaotic...'

Okay, so nothing earth-shattering, and perhaps 'wisdom' is a pretentious way of describing whatever we've learned in our lives. (We can't bear people who think they're wise!) Yet – offered humbly – other people's wisdom can be helpful. After all, we like aphorisms that we can remember and recite: pithy sayings that encapsulate certain kinds of wisdom and provide us with a context within which to make sense of our own experience. These snippets of wisdom reassure us that other people have been through similar experiences, and sometimes, gently, these snippets offer us ways forward.

Counsellors and other professionals have wisdom. Sharing that wisdom is a skill.

11

CREATIVITY AND CHAOS

'In its positive guise,' writes Peterson (2018), 'chaos is possibility itself, the source of ideas, the mysterious realm of gestation and birth. As a negative force, it's the impenetrable darkness of a cave and the accident by the side of the road' (p.41).

Writing this book has, self-evidently, been an example of creativity emerging out of my own chaos. Some people write, some make art or music, some set up organisations, some put their creative energies into propagating ideas: different people channel their chaos in different ways. And the chapters in this book have described a variety of creative possibilities emerging out of young people's chaos: Maya finally allowing her artwork (and her smile) into an uncertain relationship; Alison discovering her anger as an antidote to the bullying she experiences; Lennon developing a new-found curiosity about himself; Zak learning to imagine again; The Daisies emerging from a desultory youth centre; Alwyn beginning to find his voice after a lifetime of silence; a group of teachers and teaching assistants managing to keep thinking together despite the chaos around them; James beginning to contemplate the possibility of apologising in order to move on; and David perhaps starting to believe that he might be okay... These are all examples of chaos leading to some kind of personal creativity, the creativity of everyday life, the creativity of what Winnicott (1971) calls 'being alive'.

What enables these creative possibilities to emerge is when young people are able to acknowledge and think about their particular experience of chaos from the security of a containing relationship. For this to happen, the professionals offering that containment have to feel contained themselves. Returning to work after the death of our daughter, I was able to think about and make better sense of things with the support of my supervisor. Without her containment, I might well have become a liability because sometimes professionals have to stay with the chaos, with the unknown; they have to sit with the uncertainty, unsure sometimes where the conversation needs to go, unable to take away a young person's despair or feelings of worthlessness. It may be tempting to reach for a technique or for an activity, yet sometimes it's important simply to be alongside a young person, attuned to that young person's uncertainty, helping him or her to bear the chaos, trusting that something new will emerge, some previously 'unthought known' (Bollas 1987).

'What do you think I should do?' asks Jackson.

His father's in prison, his mother's depressed and lives with a violent, drug-dealing boyfriend, his two younger brothers are both severely autistic and he's just discovered that his girlfriend of a few months is pregnant. A story like Jackson's may sound unlikely, yet there are plenty of young people with equally – if not more – overwhelming stories. Sometimes I struggle to imagine what Jackson's life might be like.

'What do you think I should do?'

I could use a simple technique, turning the question back on him, 'What do *you* think you should do, Jackson?' I could suggest an activity, inviting him – for example – to show me his life using the pebbles in the bowl on my table to represent people or situations. Neither of these responses would be bad ideas; both might yield interesting results. But both might be ways of avoiding the chaos in Jackson's life; both might be ways of putting myself out of my own misery if his situation is making me uncomfortable. I don't have an answer to his question 'What do you think I should do?' I wish I did. I wish I could make his life better, but I can't.

When chaos strikes and life feels impossible, our attachments sustain us, whether they're attachments to people, to pets, to religions, to photographs... They soothe and comfort us, helping us to survive the worst times. However, there are plenty of young people like Jackson who appear to have no positive attachments, no good internal objects to fall back on in their lives: no supportive family relationships, no reliable friends, no good memories. So, because they must attach to something, they attach instead to drugs, or alcohol, or self-harming, or gang life: all of them ways of surviving, however destructive they may happen to be.

I'm not his parent or his friend, but Jackson still manages to come to our sessions most weeks. He knows that I keep our conversations to myself, that I don't prescribe cheap, unrealistic solutions, that I'm interested in him and that I like him: indeed, that we like each other. Being alongside him once a week in the swirling chaos of his life may not seem like much, but I think our sessions steady him, giving him time to think.

So when he asks, 'What do you think I should do?' I could take my own advice from the previous chapter and answer, 'Well in my experience...', but on this occasion I think it's important simply to acknowledge the seeming impossibility of things.

'I don't know, Jackson.'

Some young people would need a much more definite steer

than this or they'd lose faith in an overly passive counsellor who 'just listens' and never suggests anything, never says what he's thinking. But rather than offer him a steer, my judgment on this occasion is that he won't panic if I don't have the answer to his question. He knows me well enough. Our relationship is solid enough. Rather, I imagine that it'll be a relief to know that this adult whom he respects is no cleverer or wiser than he is. It'll probably be a relief to know that the seeming impossibility of his life is real, that he's not exaggerating or being stupid.

Creativity emerges out of the relationship between chaos and attachment, the unpredictability of incipient chaos and the predictability of secure attachment. 'To create something,' writes Josephine Klein (1987), 'we need chaos, but we also need order' (p.288).

Jackson and I sit in silence, thinking.

Eventually he says, 'I think I need to talk with Tasha about whether she wants to keep the baby.'

And I tell him that this sounds like a really good idea.

Describing her husband's life as president, Michelle Obama (2018) might be describing the jobs of many professionals who work with young people:

> He'd be blamed for things he couldn't control, pushed to solve frightening problems in faraway nations, expected to plug a hole at the bottom of the ocean. His job, it seemed, was to take the chaos and metabolize it somehow into calm leadership – every day of the week, every week of the year. (p.342)

Working with young people, professionals also feel the weight of impossible expectations, unable to do it all by themselves but needing to provide enough of a context that allows young people to come up with their own creative solutions. Sometimes – as with Jackson – that context needs to be quite low-key, while at other times (as I described in Chapter 9) it needs to be more deliberately 'enlivening' (Alvarez 1992).

Millie looks bewildered and pale, her hair all over the place. Her eyes are mascara smudges. 'I'm falling to bits!' she says.

Out of the blue, her boyfriend has broken up with her. She didn't see it coming and can't understand why. Nothing makes sense any longer. *She* no longer makes sense. 'I thought he loved me... Don't understand... Everything we had... Don't get it... He never said anything... Can't believe this is happening...'

We learn to make sense of ourselves and *not* fall to bits as we make relationships, as we experience ourselves mirrored back, recognised and contained by other people. Out of these experiences we develop a cumulative sense of who we are. As our anger is acknowledged, for example, so it becomes part of us. As our jokes provoke laughter, so we become funny. As our love is reciprocated, so we become loving (Luxmoore 2008). And so on.

Without that mirroring experience, we don't know who we are. Like Millie, we may invest massively in one particular mirror, but then when it's taken away or breaks up with us, we fall to bits. Without her boyfriend, she no longer makes sense to herself. She can't think. Her sentences are short, stuttering, disconnected, jumping from one thing to another. Kohut (1971) would describe the 'fragmentation' that occurs when the relationships or 'selfobjects' we absorb and upon which our sense of self is derived are lost in some way, like Millie's relationship with her boyfriend. We feel as if we're breaking down, as if we're fragmenting or 'falling to bits'. Bion (1967) describes the 'attacks on linking' that take place when the chaotic part of our personality interferes with our verbal thinking. We can no longer find the words or think clearly; we can no longer say or know what we mean.

My guess is that this isn't the first time in her life that Millie's felt like this. If adolescence is a recapitulation of infancy (Jones 1922) with adolescent experiences re-stimulating old, unresolved infantile anxieties, then her boyfriend's split from her now will probably be an unconscious reminder of earlier splits in her life. And Millie's parents *did* split up when she was four years old. So although break-ups are always upsetting, her sense of 'falling to bits' now might be because this latest event has tapped into uncertainties about herself that were always there.

We sit together as, little by little, she re-gathers herself. I try to help her join up her rational thoughts and irrational feelings, her past and her present, how she feels privately and how she must behave publicly. We're linking, always linking, linking thoughts and feelings, the conscious and the unconscious… Steve Jobs famously remarked, 'Creativity is just connecting things' (Wolf 1996). Slowly, Millie's connecting herself together again, so that she can finish our session and go back out into the world as a competent person able to catch the bus, get off at the correct stop and walk home. But over time, it'll be important for us to explore the split that happened when Millie was four years old, that old chaos re-stimulated now by her boyfriend's decision to leave: those old feelings of abandonment, that sense of things falling to bits, and all the rage and fear and confusion and longing unspoken at that time. 'What did you *feel* like saying?' is often the most useful question a young person can be asked.

When parents split, it's hard for their children not to feel split as individuals, and it's hard for them to know what to think. The job of a professional is therefore to help join things up, listening to the chaos and trying to make better sense of it, assimilating the disparate fragments so that new thoughts and understandings can emerge. As Brandt and Eagleman (2017) write, '[c]reativity is an inherently social act' (p.30) emerging out of relationships wherein we learn to hold ideas together rather than keep everything separate. T.S. Eliot (1932) describes this well in writing about the metaphysical poets, but unfortunately differentiates between the mind of a poet and the mind of someone he chooses to call 'the ordinary man':

> When a poet's mind is perfectly equipped for its work, it is constantly amalgamating disparate experience; the ordinary man's experience is chaotic, irregular, fragmentary. The latter falls in love, or reads Spinoza, and these two experiences have nothing to do with each other, or with the noise of the typewriter or the smell of cooking; in the mind of the poet these experiences are always forming new wholes. (p.287)

What Eliot might more usefully have said is that some people are better at amalgamating disparate experiences than others. Some need more help. Some struggle through no fault of their own but because – like Millie and Jackson and other young people in this book – life has dealt them more than their fair share of misfortune. Some have received help in the past and some haven't. Some have found the confidence to ask for help, while others have received help only because their behaviour screamed so loudly, so insistently and sometimes so destructively that they couldn't be ignored.

In trying to help and in trying to understand, there's always a need for professionals to wonder with each young person, 'Where's the chaos? Where is it coming from? How's it manifested? How can it be contained and how might it eventually become something creative in this young person's life?'

12

ENDPIECE

I began this book by outlining very briefly the story of our daughter's death as an example of 'external' chaos erupting out of nowhere. I want to end with a story about chaos erupting between Julia and myself.

She was, of course, the most wonderfully kind, beautiful person. And she was feisty!

A book of mine had just been published and it was the morning of the launch, to be held later that day on the lawns of an Oxford college. Lots of people would be there. Julia was 16, and because she was friendly and good at maths, she was in charge of selling the books.

But she needed to get off to school that morning and I needed to check my emails before going to work. Time was getting on, we were both in danger of being late, yet still she was upstairs on the family computer and showed no signs of finishing.

She didn't tell me what she was doing. Later, I found out that she'd decided that those people buying books at the launch might need receipts, and so – very sensibly – she was typing and printing off individual receipts. But she didn't tell me that, so I immediately became the bad guy, getting more and more irritable before eventually she retaliated and we started shouting at each other. She stormed off downstairs, slamming the front door behind her and stomping off to school.

I checked my emails, gathered my things and left the house hurriedly, going to my car.

Under the windscreen wiper was a large piece of paper on which was simply scribbled, 'You can sell your pretentious shit yourself!'

REFERENCES

Alvarez, A. (1992) *Live Company: Psychoanalytic Psychotherapy with Autistic, Borderline, Deprived and Abused Children.* Hove: Routledge.

Alvarez, A. (2012) *The Thinking Heart.* Hove: Routledge.

Bion, W.R. (1963) *Elements of Psycho-Analysis.* London: Heinemann.

Bion, W.R. (1965) *Transformations.* London: Karnac.

Bion, W.R. (1967) *Second Thoughts.* London: Heinemann.

Blakemore, S.-J. (2018) *Inventing Ourselves: The Secret Life of the Teenage Brain.* London: Transworld.

Bollas, C. (1987) *The Shadow of the Object.* London: Free Association Books.

Brandt, A. and Eagleman, D. (2017) *The Runaway Species: How Human Creativity Remakes the World.* Edinburgh: Canongate.

Cox, M. (1988) *Structuring the Therapeutic Process: Compromise with Chaos.* London: Jessica Kingsley Publishers.

Cozolino, L. (2016) *Why Therapy Works: Using Our Minds to Change Our Brains.* New York, NY, and London: Norton.

Duffell, N. (2000) *The Making of Them.* London: Lone Arrow Press.

Eagleman, D. (2016) *The Brain.* Edinburgh: Canongate.

Eigen, M. (1993) *The Electrified Tightrope.* Northvale, NJ, and London: Jason Aronson.

Eliot, T.S. (1932) 'The Metaphysical Poets.' In *Selected Essays.* London: Faber & Faber.

Eliot, T.S. (1972) *Four Quartets.* London: Faber & Faber.

Elson, M. (ed.) (1987) *The Kohut Seminars on Self Psychology and Psychotherapy with Adolescents and Young Adults.* New York, NY, and London: Norton.

Fink, B. (1997) *A Clinical Introduction to Lacanian Psychoanalysis.* Cambridge, MA, and London: Harvard University Press.

Freud, A. (2015) 'Identification with the Aggressor.' In *Selected Writings.* London: Penguin.

Freud, S. (1905) 'Jokes and Their Relation to the Unconscious.' In *The Standard Edition of the Complete Psychological Works of Sigmund Freud (Vol. 8).* London: Hogarth Press.

Freud, S. (1912) 'Recommendations to Physicians on Psycho-Analytic Technique.' In *The Standard Edition of the Complete Psychological Works of Sigmund Freud (Vol. 12).* London: Hogarth Press.

Freud, S. (1914a) 'On Narcissism: An Introduction.' In *The Standard Edition of the Complete Psychological Works of Sigmund Freud (Vol. 14).* London: Hogarth Press.

Freud, S. (1914b) 'Remembering, Repeating and Working-Through.' In *The Standard Edition of the Complete Psychological Works of Sigmund Freud (Vol. 12).* London: Hogarth Press.

Freud, S. (1920) 'Beyond the Pleasure Principle.' In *The Standard Edition of the Complete Psychological Works of Sigmund Freud (Vol. 18).* London: Hogarth Press.

Freud, S. (1923) 'The Ego and the Id.' In *The Standard Edition of the Complete Psychological Works of Sigmund Freud (Vol. 19).* London: Hogarth Press.

Gathorne-Hardy, J. (1977) *The Public School Phenomenon.* London: Faber & Faber.

Golding, W. (1954) *Lord of the Flies.* London: Penguin.

Haslam, N. (2016) 'Concept creep: Psychology's expanding concepts of harm and pathology.' *Psychological Enquiry 27,* 1, 1–17. doi:10.1080/1047 840X.2016.1082418.

Hill, D. (2015) *Affect Regulation Theory: A Clinical Model.* New York, NY, and London: Norton.

Holloway, R. (2008) *Between the Monster and the Saint.* Edinburgh: Canongate.

Holmes, J. (2001) *The Search for the Secure Base: Attachment Theory and Psychotherapy.* Hove: Brunner-Routledge.

Jersild, A.T. (1955) *When Teachers Face Themselves.* New York, NY: Teachers College Press.

Jones, E. (1922) 'Some problems of adolescence.' *British Journal of Psychoanalysis 13,* 31–47.

Kierkegaard, S. (2015) *The Concept of Anxiety.* New York, NY, and London: Norton.

King, S. (2018) *The Body.* New York, NY: Simon and Schuster. (Original work published 1982).

Klein, J. (1987) *Our Need For Others and Its Roots in Infancy.* London: Routledge.

Klein, M. (1946) 'Notes on some schizoid mechanisms.' *The International Journal of Psycho-Analysis 27,* 99–110.

Kohut, H. (1971) *The Analysis of the Self: A Systematic Approach to the Psychoanalytic Treatment of Narcissistic Personality Disorders.* New York, NY: International Universities Press.

Kristeva, J. (1982) *Powers of Horror.* New York, NY, and Chichester: Columbia University Press.

Kübler-Ross, E. (1969) *On Death and Dying.* New York, NY: Simon and Schuster.

Kurtz, A. and Coetzee, J.M. (2015) *The Good Story: Exchanges on Truth, Fiction and Psychotherapy.* London: Harvill Secker.

Lacan, J. (1966) *Ecrits: A Selection.* New York, NY, and London: Norton.

Luxmoore, N. (2006) *Working with Anger and Young People.* London: Jessica Kingsley Publishers.

Luxmoore, N. (2008) *Feeling Like Crap.* London: Jessica Kingsley Publishers.

Luxmoore, N. (2009) *Young People in Love and in Hate.* London: Jessica Kingsley Publishers.

Luxmoore, N. (2014) *School Counsellors Working with Young People and Staff: A Whole-School Approach.* London: Jessica Kingsley Publishers.

Luxmoore, N. (2017) *Practical Supervision for Counsellors Who Work with Young People.* London: Jessica Kingsley Publishers.

Luxmoore, N. (2019) *The Art of Working with Anxious, Antagonistic Adolescents: Ways Forward for Frontline Professionals.* London: Jessica Kingsley Publishers.

Mawson, C. (1994) 'Containing Anxiety in Work with Damaged Children.' In A. Obholzer and V.Z. Roberts (eds.) *The Unconscious at Work: Individual and Organisational Stress in the Human Services.* London: Routledge.

May, R. (1977) *The Meaning of Anxiety.* New York, NY, and London: Norton.

Molino, A. (1997) *Freely Associated: Encounters in Psychoanalysis.* London: Free Association Books.

Mollon, P. (2002) *Shame and Jealousy: The Hidden Turmoils.* London: Karnac.

Moreno, J.L. (1961) 'The Role Concept: A Bridge Between Psychiatry and Sociology.' In J. Fox (ed.) *The Essential Moreno.* New York, NY: Springer.

Mowles, C. (2015) *Managing in Uncertainty.* Abingdon: Routledge.

Murphy, A. (2017) *Out of This World: Suicide Examined.* London: Karnac.

Music, G. (2014) *The Good Life.* London and New York, NY: Routledge.

Nietzsche, F. (1961) *Thus Spoke Zarathustra.* London: Penguin.

Obama, M. (2018) *Becoming.* London: Viking.

Obholzer, A. and Roberts, V.Z. (eds.) (1994) *The Unconscious at Work: Individual and Organisational Stress in the Human Services.* London: Routledge.

Peterson, J.B. (2018) *12 Rules for Life: An Antidote to Chaos.* London: Allen Lane.

Phillips, A. (2012) *Missing Out: In Praise of the Unlived Life.* London: Hamish Hamilton.

Phillips, A. (2019) *Paying Attention.* London: Penguin.

Reiner, R. (Director) (1986) *Stand by Me* [Motion picture]. USA: Columbia Pictures.

Renton, A. (2017) *Stiff Upper Lip.* London: Weidenfeld & Nicolson.

Riley, D. (2019) *Time Lived, Without Its Flow.* London: Picador.

Rothschild, B. (2000) *The Body Remembers: The Psychophysiology of Trauma and Trauma Treatment.* New York, NY: Norton.

Rowling, J.K. (1999) *Harry Potter and the Prisoner of Azkaban.* London: Bloomsbury.

Sartre, J.-P. (1943) *Being and Nothingness.* Paris: Editions Gallimard.

Schafer, R. (2003) *Bad Feelings.* London: Karnac.

Spring, C. (2016) *Recovery Is My Best Revenge.* Huntingdon: Carolyn Spring Publishing.

Steiner, J. (1993) *Psychic Retreats: Pathological Organisations in Psychotic, Neurotic and Borderline Patients.* London and New York, NY: Routledge.

Stern, D.N. (1985) *The Interpersonal World of the Infant.* New York, NY: Basic Books.

Storr, A. (1972) *The Dynamics of Creation.* London: Secker and Warburg.

Van der Kolk, B. (2014) *The Body Keeps the Score.* London: Allen Lane.

Waddell, M. (2018) *On Adolescence.* London: Karnac.

Waits, T. (1999) 'What's He Building?' [Song]. From *Mule Variations.* Jalma Music.

Wieland-Burston, J. (1992) *Chaos and Order in the World of the Psyche.* London: Routledge.

Williams, W.C. (1976) *Selected Poems.* London: Penguin.

Wilson, R.Z. (2014) *Neuroscience for Counsellors.* London: Jessica Kingsley Publishers.

Winnicott, D.W. (1964) *The Child, the Family, and the Outside World.* London: Pelican.

Winnicott, D.W. (1965) *The Maturational Processes and the Facilitating Environment.* London: Hogarth Press.

Winnicott, D.W. (1971) *Playing and Reality.* London: Routledge.

Winnicott, D.W. (1986) 'Delinquency as a Sign of Hope.' In *Home Is Where We Start From.* New York, NY: Norton.

Winnicott, D.W. (1988) *Human Nature.* London: Free Association Books.

Winnicott, D.W. (1989) *Psycho-Analytic Explorations.* London: Karnac.

Winnicott, D.W. (1996) *Thinking About Children.* London: Karnac.

Wolf, G. (1996) *Steve Jobs: The next insanely great thing* [Interview]. www.wired.com/1996/02/jobs-2.

Yalom, I.D. (1980) *Existential Psychotherapy.* New York, NY: Basic Books.

Yeats, W.B. (1961) *Selected Poetry.* London: Macmillan.

INDEX